D1607364

"Brilliant and addictive, *Teen Writer's Guide* is a must-read for every serious aspiring teen writer!"

—Kathryn Purdie, #1 *New York Times* bestselling author of *Burning Glass* and *Bone Crier's Moon*

"*Teen Writer's Guide*…is easy-to-read, entertaining (a must for teenagers), organized in a logical and easy-to-follow format, and best of all, contains language, instructions, and activities that are completely within the capabilities of my students.

Finally! I have a textbook that I can actually use! I am so excited for this book—its organization and content fits perfectly with the order and structure of my class, and its core connections make it even more teacher-friendly.

There is a dire need for Creative Writing textbooks in secondary education, and I am excited that now I—and many other Creative Writing teachers—will have a textbook that will help us teach this amazing subject."

—Adena Campbell, High School Creative Writing Teacher

"Chock full of great tips, writing exercises, and plenty of humor, this is a must-read for the young author!"

—Jessica Day George, *New York Times* **bestselling author of the Tuesdays at the Castle series**

"Jennifer Jenkins' *Teen Writer's Guide* is the roadmap I wish I'd had when I was an aspiring teen writer. It's funny, accessible, and best of all, chock full of smart tips to help young writers become better."

—Rosalyn Eves, Author of *Blood Rose Rebellion* **and Creative Writing Professor/PhD**

teen
writer's
GUIDE

YOUR ROAD MAP TO WRITING

Jennifer Jenkins

OWL HOLLOW PRESS

Educators and librarians, for a variety of videos and other teaching resources, please visit owlhollowpress.com and authorjenniferjenkins.com.

Library of Congress Control Number: 2020930586
ISBN 978-1-945654-41-1 (paperback)
ISBN 978-1-945654-42-8 (e-book)

TEEN WRITER'S GUIDE: YOUR ROAD MAP TO WRITING/ Jenkins. 1st ed.

Edited by Olivia Swenson
Cover Design by Propergraphic

www.owlhollowpress.com

Owl Hollow Press, LLC, Springville, UT 84663

*To the creative teen writer: You are brave and powerful.
Change the world and write.*

To Margie, Jo, Tahsha, and Lois: I love you. It has been an honor.

CONTENTS

Introduction

I was nine years old when I first discovered my love of stories. As a military kid (notice I didn't say "brat"), my life seemed like one giant road trip. Like popcorn on a hot stove, my family jumped across the US, moving anywhere Uncle Sam wanted us to go. Couple that with my parents' passion for house flipping and overall spontaneous nature, and by the time I turned sixteen, we had moved eighteen times.

Chew on that for just a second.

My parents didn't keep track, but I chronicled every new school, every house, every sprinkler system installed, and every friend left behind.

When I was nine, we drove across the country from Utah to Florida. Imagine 2,328 miles, an undisclosed number of gas station apple pies, and approximately 34 hours in a car. My dad decided to break up the monotony by retelling a story from a fantasy novel he'd just read.

Travel Log Note: This was back in the Jurassic Period when we didn't have tablets with endless viewing and gaming options at our fingertips. No cell phones, no TVs in the car to play DVDs, no DVDs for that matter… I think you get my point. We had the radio, the occasional Neil Diamond cassette tape, and the scenery outside the car window to keep us entertained. Let's all gasp at the horror together, shall we?

Turns out, my dear old dad had a talent for telling stories. He had us on the edge of our seats for hours. And I do mean the edge of our seats, because seatbelts were optional back then. Over time, Dad's stories morphed from books he'd read into hybrid creations that starred my siblings and I in leading roles. I found myself battling dragons, wielding magical objects, and saving the world from evil—all from the backseat of a brown 1985 Colt Vista. Dad would talk himself hoarse and then we'd beg him to continue the story.

In a way, I think my father's stories were the beginning of my career as a storyteller. They gave me permission to create in a way I'd never thought possible.

In school, my writing was either regurgitated fact or technically driven. It was all reports, research papers, and essays, but never any short stories, poems, or longer fiction. I hated reading and writing (for reasons I'll get to soon enough). I always got good grades because, if my military lifestyle taught me anything, it was how to be a master chameleon. I learned how to produce the words/answers that my teachers wanted. It was the equivalent of "coloring inside the lines."

But how could I be happy merely coloring inside the lines when in my head I was building worlds and creating epic adventures? When we got our first home computer, I had files filled with half-finished stories that were all suspiciously similar to *Anne of Green Gables*. (Google it. I promise it's good.)

By the time I hit junior high, I had caged my creativity, shaking a proverbial finger at it and telling it to behave. The concept of reading novels for enjoyment didn't even register for me.

> **Travel Log Note**: I did write sappy poetry in a leather-bound journal, because the stories had to go somewhere.

I graduated from high school and studied history in college. It seemed I couldn't escape my love of oral storytelling. I devoured lectures from professors on war, culture, religion, politics… any story I could get my hands on. The monster within craved the stories I'd denied it throughout junior high and high school, and I found myself sitting in on classes I wasn't even registered for. For me, history cracked open a window and let stories and creativity back into my life.

I found myself daydreaming again.

But I still believed writing had to be scholarly. I was a good writer but thought if I really wanted to write, I needed to start with history articles for scholarly journals. I hoped to eventually obtain the *street cred* to do something really wild… like write history textbooks.

Yawn… Right?

Long story short, I didn't give myself permission to write creatively and read for pleasure until I was about twenty-one. I'd finished my bachelor's degree and was toying with the idea of going back to obtain a master's when I stumbled upon a little-known book called *Harry Potter and the Sorcerer's Stone*.

Okay, stumbled might not be the right word. Half the world had read the book by the time I picked it up. My older brother practically shoved it into my hands and said, "READ THIS!" At first, I resisted. I was contemplating a master's degree, for crying out loud. If a book didn't delve into the mysteries of the human condition blah blah blah, I turned my nose up at it.

After I met Harry, it was as though the dam holding back my creative juices broke.

I became a woman obsessed.

Flash forward three years later to the Barnes and Noble book release party for the *Order of the Phoenix* where I won the costume contest dressed as Dobby the house elf. Talk about a transformation.

I read literally hundreds of novels after I discovered Harry Potter before attempting to write my first official book at the age of twenty-five. It was a tantalizing education and I lived vicariously through some of my favorite characters during that time. Those were very good years.

Today, I have several published novels under my belt. I am a founding board member for a non-profit organization that advocates for teen literacy. I am a creator of Teen Author Boot Camp, one of the nation's most successful writers conferences exclusively for teens, attracting nearly a thousand bright and driven young writers from across the US every year. I put on a summer writing camp for teens at a local university. I've spent time in countless high schools and junior highs, from New England to the Deep South to west of the Rockies, talking with teens about the benefits of reading and writing.

It's been a wild ride and a very different road than I planned to travel back in my college days. If I could change one element of my growing-up years, it wouldn't be moving so many times. In all honesty, I had an incredible, unique childhood! *Waves at Mom and Dad.* I would change the time I wasted as a teen trapped in the false belief that writing meant only research papers and homework.

I had a killer voice, but I didn't feel like I had permission to use it.

My mission with this book is to coax your caged voice out from hiding and provide some writing advice I would have loved when I was a teenager. If you're a wise guy, you might be connecting the dots and exclaiming, "You wrote a textbook after all!"

But you're wrong. This is a *permission* book. It's totally different.

I hereby grant permission to teens everywhere to express themselves and their ideas through writing. It's satisfying, and you might just be surprised by your own ability to create.

Writing is about the journey more than the destination. Hop in the back seat and I'll take you on a drive through the wilds of writing a story of your very own.

(Seatbelts are optional.)

1

Choosing the Right Vehicle

My parents had no idea their seventeen-year-old daughter was in Jackson Hole, sleeping on a stranger's couch above the Jackson Hole Playhouse—no idea that I'd traveled there without adult supervision. My friend Angela and I hadn't planned for our summer trip to go this way—but I suppose when you're a spontaneous, bone-headed teenager, anything is possible.

Eight Days Earlier

"My mom is going to kill me." My best friend, Angela, trails me carrying her backpack over one shoulder while hugging her prized 300-capacity CD case to her chest.

I pop the trunk of the Tercel and sigh. "You need to let a little adventure into your life."

Angela throws her backpack in on top of the tent and sleeping bags. "I swear you say that every weekend."

"I swear you need to hear it every weekend." I shut the trunk and we climb in the front seat. The atlas I had taken from my father's truck rests between us, folded into place with a map showing the Utah/Wyoming border.

"For the record, your parents are going to kill you, too," she says.

"They know where I'm going," I mumble, examining the map. Apparently there are several ways to reach Jackson Hole from our hometown in northern Utah. The trouble with a road atlas is that it doesn't have any fancy features to help you know the fastest route. The plan is simple: drive the shortest number of miles as the crow flies. Fool proof.

Travel Log Note: Can you imagine taking a road trip without Google Maps or GPS? Life before the smartphone was madness!!!

"But you didn't tell them the details," says Angela.

I'd told my parents the highlights. That we were going to visit another friend working a summer job in Jackson Hole, Wyoming. I may have implied that we were traveling with Angela's mom. And I'm sure it was assumed that we had a place to stay during our mountain adventure.

I hand Angela the atlas and put the car in gear. After a quick tank of gas—it only took about $9.50 to fill 'er up—and the purchase of two quarts of oil, we are on the road.

Why the oil?

My old car burned oil like a fire burns lighter fluid. I'd become a master with a dipstick and averaged about a quart a week.

Travel Log Note: We call this detail foreshadowing. We'll be talking all about it in Chapter 5.

The drive to Jackson takes almost two hours longer than I think it should. We fill our time shout-singing the lyrics to our favorite metal songs and eating Red Vines. I'm not certain if it's the drastic change in altitude as we climb the Teton Pass or the candy overload that has me nauseated, but I can't help but sigh in relief as we descend into the Jackson Hole Valley.

The week passes in a blur of unexpected chaos. We quickly discover that we can't camp on the side of the road, and the local campground charges insane rates. Armed with only $50 dollars to my name, we make *friends with some actors at the Jackson Hole Playhouse and end up crashing in the tiny apartment above the Playhouse for a week. I love the theater, but I hope I never see* Big River *again.*

The money goes quickly and by day five we are forced to quite literally sing for our supper (more on that later). Worse still, my car is acting up, the temperature gauge constantly flirts with the red, and I have a sickening feeling in the pit of my stomach every time I think about the drive home.

On our last day, I add a fresh quart of oil to the Tercel and we begin our steep journey up the Teton Pass with just enough money for one tank of gas.

My little car soon becomes a real-life analogy for The Little Engine that Could. *Actually, it is more like* The Little Engine that Can't Even. *The temperature of my engine climbs with every passing minute, and in some places it is so steep, first gear in the Tercel barely has us moving. My palms are slick with sweat as cars speed past us on the left.*

We round a tight bend, just before the summit of the pass, and I slam on my brakes, killing the necessary momentum to make it to the top.

Blocking our path, like something out of a C.S. Lewis nightmare, stands the largest, most aggressive moose I've ever seen. As if my car knows it has lost the battle with the mountain, it sputters and dies, steam rising from the hood. The ears of the moose lie flat, reminding me of an aggressive, snarling dog. It charges toward us, swinging its impressive antlers from side to side, then stops directly in front of my car.

"I think I've had my fill of adventure," I say, with no clue how we'll get out of this one.

Testing Story Concepts

I could fill the pages of an entire book on teenage recklessness describing my adventures in Jackson Hole that summer—I'd call it *Cautionary Tales of a Teenage Optimist,* or maybe *How To Lose Your Life in 10 Days,* or my personal favorite, *From the Seat of the Tercel It Was Clear the Moose Was Male.*

There is nothing wrong with being spontaneous, but a little fore-thought can save you a lot of trouble in both traveling and creative writing.

Say you decided to take a cross-country trip. You'd definitely want a reliable car to get you to your destination. You'd probably check your tires, change your oil, survey the engine, etc. You may even replace your windshield wipers just to make sure you aren't swimming in bug guts by mile 200.

If your vehicle is a piece of crap like mine was, you might consider buying a new one. Most manufacturers today have websites that allow you to completely personalize your car. With the click of a mouse, you can choose the make, model, color, tires, sound system, interior, and special features of your vehicle. You can "build" your dream car without even leaving your living room!

Very rarely does a writer sit down at a desk and declare, "I'm going to write a book today!" Usually story ideas come from sources of inspiration. It may be a song, an eye-opening tropical vacation, or maybe even a re-markable person in our lives. Perhaps you've had a moment like J.K. Rowling where a character simply walks into your head.

I once wrote an entire novel after see-ing a picture of Manarola, Italy. I re-member thinking "A story happens here," and then I let my mind wander over the possibilities. Charac-ters and ideas for plot points and scenes danced like visions of

Manarola, Italy

sugarplums in my head. Pirates, curses, true love—this book was going to have it all. I set out to write that very day. This project would become my masterpiece.

I cranked out a few chapters and then discovered that my plot was not as solid as I'd originally thought. The middle of the story lagged and the ending didn't quite satisfy.

The problem: I'd started without proper preparation, without growing and stretching my idea into something big and strong enough to carry my reader across the span of a full novel. In my hurry to get writing, I missed some really cool opportunities to make the story great.

When my literary agent emailed me with feedback for the manuscript, it was like taking a sharp pin to a shiny red balloon. This was supposed to be my masterpiece, remember? My agent said the idea had potential but suggested I go back to the drawing board.

I hadn't been able to translate my initial inspiration into something great.

It crushed me.

Was I wrong to act on this new idea? Were the gods of inspiration chomping on theater popcorn and laughing at me from the sky?

No.

I firmly believe when we are given inspiration we should act. But before every great creation there is often a moment when the artist, writer, creator has to stop and really think and emotionally process what they want to make. For a painter, that might entail staring at a blank canvas while visualizing the final product in their mind. For a musician, it might mean playing around to find the right key signature to express the desired mood of a song. It may be the deep breath a sculptor takes when he is only fingertip deep in clay.

This pause in creation should never be confused with doubt. Rather, it is a moment to gather the courage necessary to create something we know has meaning—something that is an extension of ourselves. As artists, we must take a moment to challenge our ideas since they are the vehicles that will get us where we want to go.

Here are a few important questions that writers should know the answers to *before* they set out to write a novel. Consider this a way to take your awesome idea on a test drive before you hop in and take off! It is guaranteed to save you time and heartache later on.

Question #1: Who would enjoy reading this type of book?

If you plan to share this novel with others in the future, knowing your intended audience and genre can be beneficial both in plotting and writing your novel.

The easiest way to determine the audience of a novel is to look at the age of the main character. Most young people like to read books about characters that are just a little older than their current age. For example, if you're writing a book meant for children 8-12 years old, your main character will likely be 12-14 years old. The publishing world calls this age group a Middle Grade audience.

If you're writing for teens, your main character will probably be somewhere between 15-18 years old. The publishing world refers to readers twelve and older as Young Adult readers.

If you're writing for adults, your characters will most likely be eighteen years or older.

> **Travel Log Note**: You may find it interesting that almost 60% of young adult book readers are actually adults. There's something about coming-of-age stories that appeals to a wide-range of readers.

Once you know the age range, it's easier to nail down your project's genre. The term "genre" is French for "sort or style." From this list of fiction genres, determine under which category your idea might fall.

- Action and Adventure (think Indiana Jones)
- Dystopian (messed up society from the future)
- Fantasy (magical objects or people/mythical creatures)
- Fairytale Retelling
- Contemporary or General Fiction (present day, our world)
- Graphic Novel
- Historical Fiction
- Horror
- Humor

- Mystery
- Paranormal (think ghosts, vampires)
- Romance
- Suspense/Thriller
- Science Fiction (fantastical technology/world explained by science instead of magic)
- Urban Fantasy (Magic set in present day)

The story about my Jackson Hole summer would be classified as Young Adult Contemporary. Young Adult, due to the age of the protagonist, and Contemporary, because it takes place relatively in the here and now.

> **Travel Log Note**: "Protagonist" is a fancy way of referring to the main character. We will discuss this more in Chapter 2.

If you're not certain what genre your idea falls under, consider other books that might be similar to your idea.

For example, if your idea involves teens battling a corrupt government in the future, you might compare it to books such as *The Maze Runner* or *The Hunger Games*. These books are considered Dystopian.

What about books that feel as though they belong to more than one genre?

No sweat! Say you're writing a fantasy novel intended for teens and you plan to include romance… you'd call that a Young Adult Fantasy. No need to include the "romance" label because the primary genre is Fantasy. In this case, Romance is considered a sub-genre. If you called it a Young Adult Romance, your readers might be in for a big surprise when a fire-breathing dragon eats your main character's best friend in the opening chapter.

Project labels can sometimes scare writers or make them feel as though they are confined in their writing, but that doesn't need to be the case. Knowing your genre is less about limiting your writing and more about understanding what those who read your genre love. It also helps to know what other people are writing so you can try to keep your story original.

Readers of Middle Grade tend to gravitate toward books with humor and gobble up supernatural and magical themes. So if you're writing a story about a ten-year-old whose main conflict is moving to a new school, you might consider adding some good humor to the project. As for teens and adults, no matter the genre, they usually appreciate some element of romance, even if the book isn't primarily about building romantic attachments.

By answering the question "Who would read this type of book?" we might stumble onto the answer of another question: Who would most likely not enjoy this story? Recognizing that you're writing for a specific audience means you don't have to try to please everyone.

For example, if you're into historical fiction, don't feel pressured to write about magic systems, space travel, or something else you think other people will find "cool."

You know you have a good novel idea if it feels like something you'd die to get your hands on as a reader. You're going to need that enthusiasm for the story to see you through to the end.

Question #2: What character should narrate this book?

You may assume your main character will narrate your new story idea, but in literature that isn't always the case. In *The Book Thief* by Markus Zusak the narrator happens to be Death. (Cool, right?) The Sherlock Holmes novels by Arthur Conan Doyle were narrated not by Sherlock himself, but his righthand man, Dr. Watson. Take the time to decide who is the best person to tell your story.

You may be interested in having more than one narrator. In my *Nameless* trilogy, both the hero and heroine take turns narrating the story. Having multiple narrators can be wonderful because we get to see the story through both of their perspectives. The downside to having multiple narrators is that you have to work extra hard to make sure your narrators don't sound like the same person.

I've read exceptional books by authors who have had as many as five narrators, but again, this is extremely hard to do well. A good example is Leigh Bardugo's mind-blowing novel *The Six of Crows*. Each of her narrating characters *speak* with a distinct voice.

Travel Log Note: More on this when we discuss Characters and Narrative Voice in Chapter 2.

Even if my Jackson Hole story wasn't meant to be autobiographical, I'd still consider my character the narrator, mostly because I think it would be vital that she/I (wow, feeling rather meta right now) would need to be present through all of the action. Much of the humor of the story will translate better coming from her/my perspective. Also, it is a common practice in the Young Adult Contemporary genre for the lead heroine to tell the story.

Question #3: What is the best point of view and tense for this idea?

If you're not big on Language Arts, don't panic! I'll break this down in the most simple and painless way possible.

Point of view (POV) describes the angle from which a story is told. Basically, we're talking about *how* the narrator or storyteller tells the story. Are they watching the story like a movie? Are they in the story, acting as one of the characters? Are they talking to the reader directly? It all depends on their point of view. It's wise to consider the most effective viewpoint to use before setting out on your writing adventure. New writers tend to "shift lanes" with POV without realizing it, which can be very confusing to the reader.

The same can be true with tense. Once you decide whether you're writing in past tense or present tense, stick with it! This can be difficult if the book you're currently reading is written in past tense, and the book you're currently writing is written in present tense. It's so important to stay consistent, otherwise you distract the reader from the story. I often encourage young writers to experiment writing in both past and present tense to see which feels the best to you and to your story.

In the English language, we use three types of POV: first person (I screamed), second person (you screamed), and third person (he/she screamed). Especially in fiction, first and third person POV are by far the most common, so I'll start with those.

First Person POV

First person POV is narrated from the perspective of a character, usually the main character.

Pros: Allows readers to see inside the character's head and heart. It is often easier to show personality in narration with this POV.

Cons: The reader is limited to the knowledge and personal experience of the main character.

Let's look at some examples of using first person POV in both past and present tense.

Example of first person past tense: *I shifted the car into first gear, praying the sputtering engine could carry us to the summit.*

Example of first person present tense: *I shift the car into first gear, praying the sputtering engine can carry us to the summit.*

The difference between present and past tense is all in the verbs. In this case "shifted" and "could" (past tense) change to "shift" and "can" (present).

Am I losing you yet? If you're on the verge of jumping out of this moving vehicle, grab that little handle above your window and hold on for just a second. I promise we're almost there. Let's look at third person POV.

Third Person POV

A close third person POV reads as though looking over the shoulder of the main character. If you zoom out, you can also use what some call "omniscient" third person POV, where the story is told by an all-seeing/all-knowing eye who knows what everyone is doing, thinking, and feeling. (Never to be confused with the Eye of Sauron. *hee hee*)

Pros: Close third person can read a lot like first person, using the character's thoughts and turn of phrase. It also lends itself well to having multiple narrators.

Cons: That little bit of extra distance from the main character—especially if you are using omniscient third person—can keep the reader from identifying as closely with the character since they are not riding around inside the character's head.

Example of third person past tense: *She shifted the car into first gear, praying the sputtering engine could carry them to the summit.*

Example of third person present tense: *She shifts the car into first gear, praying the sputtering engine can carry them to the summit.*

I suggest writing a scene using each of these POVs. Decide what feels best to you. Play with your tenses. Just know that once your commit to a POV and tense, it's important that you stick with it throughout the course of the book. Remember, unintentionally "changing lanes" confuses your reader.

Second Person POV

Second person POV is written as though you, the reader, are the narrator. Instead of "I" or "she," it is "you" telling the story.

While it is very uncommon for a novel to be written in second person, it can be a creative choice that is quite engaging if done well. And that is the key problem—it's extremely hard to do well. I think one of the best modern examples of second person narration is *The Night Circus* by Erin Morgenstern. In this excerpt, notice how she is address "you" the reader:

> *"What kind of circus is only open at night?" people ask. No one has a proper answer, yet as dusk approaches there is a substantial crowd of spectators gathering outside the gates.*
>
> *You are amongst them, of course. Your curiosity got the better of you, as curiosity is wont to do. You stand in the fading light, the scarf around your neck pulled up against the chilly evening breeze, waiting to see for yourself exactly what kind of circus only opens once the sun sets.*

Pros: So long as the reader can relate to the scenario, the narration feels intimate and personal to the reader.

Cons: It can be confusing and can become exhausting to the reader. Many people simply don't like it in more than small doses. And if the reader doesn't relate to the scenario, it can actually distance them from the story, rather than drawing them in.

Consider your story and the pros and cons of each POV before deciding how you plan to narrate your story. You may want to take the story out for a test drive practicing each POV to see which feels most natural. As I said before, jumping POV within a scene and even a chapter will confuse your reader, so it's important to plan ahead and stick to your decision.

Question #4: What is the main conflict of the story?

Good stories have one main struggle or conflict that carries readers through the entire book/series. Great stories have many conflicts, both internal and external.

At this point, I just want you to identify the big, mother-load conflict(s). The type of conflict your story has will depend on its genre and audience.

Your main conflict is usually external. Think of some of your favorite books and films. Whether it's destroying the Death Star, surviving the Hunger Games, or winning the big game, there is an obvious external challenge that must be fought and eventually conquered. In a thriller novel, the main conflict will definitely be external. For example, capturing the serial killer or killing the homicidal beast in the woods, etc. In my Jackson Hole story, the main conflict would be finding a way to get home with the very little money in my pockets.

In romance and high drama stories, internal conflict is king. For example, the main conflict might be about forgiving someone, overcoming personal weakness, or perhaps letting go of pain and starting over.

Star Wars is a classic example of a story carrying both a strong external conflict (blowing up the Death Star) and internal conflict (Luke finding his father and confronting his deepest fears).

To test the strength of your main conflict, ask the next question…

Question #5: What is at stake if your hero/heroine fails?

The very first novel I ever wrote was a fantasy story about a girl in high school who learns she's a hunted princess from another realm ruled by the goddess Natura. When I was asked Question #5 by another author after writing the book, I'm embarrassed to admit that I didn't really have an answer. I believe I said something incredibly lame like, "She goes back home."

When nothing is at stake, your plot will run out of gas on the highway in Death Valley! Writers must provide consequences to failure. They must be prepared to dangle those consequences over the heads of their characters like a butcher's knife on a chopping block.

Let's apply this to Jackson Hole, shall we?

If I can't find a way to get my car functioning before my parents discover what I've done, I'll be forced to call them for help and admit that I took the trip under false pretenses.

This is good, but how can we make my situation even more desperate?

How about, if I can't get us home, I'll miss my grandparents' fiftieth wedding anniversary party? Maybe I'm trying to convince my folks that I'm responsible enough to spend a month in Europe, and if they discover what I've done, they'll never let me go. Or perhaps Angela is diabetic and needs to get back home for more insulin.

Do you notice how each of these extra layers of conflict raise the stakes of the story just a bit?

Keep in mind that high stakes make the victory *mean* more and will also help your story hold tension.

Travel Log Note: More on conflict and stakes coming your way in Chapter 5.

Question #6: What does my main character want more than anything else?

Throughout the course of this book, we're going to spend a lot of time talking about motivation. I can't emphasize enough how important it is for your characters to want—even better—*need* something. Make it their oxygen. Make it seem as though the world might crumble if they don't obtain it. The more desperate your character's motivation, the more intense your story.

Motivation and backstory are sisters and often play off of one another.

For example, if Jane's main goal in life is to climb Mt. Kilimanjaro, her backstory can answer the question "why" and make her desire to climb mean more. Perhaps Jane's father died climbing Kilimanjaro when she was just a baby and she believes summiting that peak would be the closest experience she'll ever have to knowing her father.

Great writers make sure that *all* prominent characters in the story have some form of motivation, especially the protagonist (main character) and antagonist (villain). By understanding what people want, a lot of other parts of the story—such as backstory—fall naturally into place.

Question #7: What is the best setting/society to provide conflict for my character(s)?

If your story idea is inspired by a character, ask yourself what kind of setting would best enhance that character. Perhaps your character is compassionate in a culture that views compassion as weakness, a male raised in a matriarchal society, or an artist living in a technology-driven world.

A good example is from the animated film *How to Train Your Dragon*. The main character, Hiccup, is the Viking chief's son. Unlike his huge, muscled father, Hiccup is a scrawny, smart inventor in a society that doesn't appreciate his worth. Add the fact that he shows mercy and eventually befriends the enemy, and you have a character rife with conflict.

Consider J.K. Rowling's world of half-bloods, mudbloods, and purebloods. How do these society distinctions create conflict in the Harry Potter novels? In Ally Condie's Matched series, the main character becomes obsessed with poems and stories in a society that has banned literature and freedom of expression.

Be careful not to settle with a setting/world that is too convenient for your main character. Easy is boring! Remember, our job as writers is to throw conflict at our main character, and you need to capitalize on every possible opportunity to do so.

Question #8: What kind of characters would be most interesting in this setting/story?

If your story idea is inspired by a setting, you have the opportunity to create dynamic, conflicted characters centered around that setting. For example, in the movie *Avatar*, the planet Pandora is filled with adventure and thrills. The native people are stronger, faster, and more agile than humans. The screenwriter, James Cameron, could have used anyone as a main character and this movie still would have been amazing simply because of the world and setting.

But instead of an average Joe, the writer introduced viewers to Jake Sully, a paraplegic ex-military operative. When Jake gains the use of his avatar and experiences running and diving through the jungle and flying on the back of a banshee, it means so much more to him than it would for someone who had a fully functioning body.

That's just good writing.

"What If" Questions: The Idea Ignition

If you find yourself struggling to answer some of the questions in the previous section, this section is for you. As an author, one of the most commonly asked questions I receive when I visit schools or speak at conventions is: "Where do you get your ideas?"

The answer can be boiled down to two simple words: "What if?"

All stories have a premise (i.e., feuding clans vying for dominance, two people falling in love, space ninjas attacking the galaxy), and all premises begin with "What If" questions.

- What if a young prince is cruel to an enchantress who then turns him into a beast until he learns to behave?
- What if a girl agrees to offer herself to the beast in exchange for her ailing father?
- What if there is a time limit for the beast to prove that he's not a monster?
- What if the girl and the beast fall in love?

I think you get my drift.

Don't plan to use all of the ideas that come out in your brainstorming session. Often writers begin by asking "What if?" to a few ideas, which spawns new ideas and they ask "What if?" to those. The process can go on and on. A good "What if?" brainstorm includes ideas that may seem absurd and even laughable, but I challenge you to turn your left-brained reasoning off for a second and let your creativity flow. Take U-turns and

JENNIFER JENKINS · 21

detours and maybe even do a little off-roading. No rules. No road maps. Just "What if?"

Remember that you are the author of this story, and you give it permission to grow into anything it wants to become.

Shall we use my Jackson Hole summer of madness as an example?

- What if our heroine reached Jackson Hole to discover she wasn't allowed to camp outside of an expensive campground or on private property?
- What if their friend didn't have a place for them to stay?
- What if our heroine met a few nice young, male actors who were in the middle of doing a production of *Big River* at the Jackson Hole Playhouse?
- What if they invited our heroine and her friend to crash on their living room couches for the duration of their visit?
- What if that apartment was really the second-story loft of the playhouse?
- What if there was a creepy thirty-year-old guy who also happened to live there?

See how fun this can be? Now lets go a little deeper. Remember, the purpose is to let your mind wander. Drop boundaries and challenge your original ideas. Those ideas don't own your story…you do!

- What if, while exploring the town, the girls decide it's a good idea to sing for coin on a busy corner to earn enough money for gas and repairs to get home?
- What if the owner of a Chuck Wagon entertainment company hears them and asks them to perform for his customers that evening?
- What if they literally sing for their supper and ride in the same covered wagons up the mountain that carried all of the guests?
- What if a hired band of teenage bandits pretended to attack the wagons on horseback while they are en route?

- What if those boys persuade the girls to join them on a midnight horseback ride?

   Travel Log Note: Believe it or not, the events of this brainstorm actually happened, proving truth often is stranger than fiction.

Once you have several pages of ideas for characters, plot, premise, etc., then I recommend going back and taking a highlighter to the good stuff that you know you want to use. It's possible—and likely—that your seemingly random ideas will lead you to some of your best story ideas.

Whether you have a clear idea for plot and character, or you're just scrambling for something to turn into a creative writing teacher for school, testing your story ideas and using "What if?" questions can push the boundaries of your creativity and help you detect potential problems. You can embark on your writing journey with confidence that your "story vehicle" has enough gas in the tank to carry you from Chapter One to The End.

Hit the Road: Story Idea Writing Prompt

Part One: Using your own story idea, take the time to write out the answers to the eight essential questions discussed in this section. *
   1. Who would enjoy reading this type of book?
   2. What character should narrate this book?
   3. What is the best point of view and tense for this idea?
   4. What is the main conflict of the story?
   5. What is at stake if your hero/heroine fails?
   6. What does my main character want more than anything else?
   7. What is the best setting/society to provide conflict for my character(s)?
   8. What kind of characters would be most interesting in this setting/story?

Part Two: Using "What if?" questions, brainstorm and challenge your story concept by asking at least fifteen of your own "What if?" questions. Be creative!

*If you are having trouble coming up with a story idea, you may consider reversing the order of these writing prompts and begin with "What if?" Start simple (i.e., What if there was a boy who loved airplanes? What if he wanted to become a pilot?) and then build from there. There are stories in everything. You may surprise yourself by what you create.

2

Characters Who are Going Places

My eyes drift shut until another bump in the road jerks me awake. Dad has Garth Brooks singing about "Friends in Low Places" on the radio, and Mom and my two siblings are probably already at the motel we're calling home tonight with our second car.

Mom will worry when we don't show for a few hours, but the mechanic took longer than we thought replacing our brakes. I'm sure Dad's beeper will start buzzing any moment.

Travel Log Note: A "beeper" or "pager" is a fancy device that pre-dates cell phones. You could call the number assigned to the beeper, and then leave a number for them to call you back. If you were really fancy, you could even leave cool messages using numbers to spell out words if read upside-down, i.e., HELLO.

I don't mind the delay. As the middle child, I am always thirsty for one-on-one time with Mom or Dad. And it's my turn to have the backseat all to myself. With no one poking me in the ribs or sticking wet fingers in my ear, I'm free to stretch out with my feet propped up against the window and my favorite down pillow under my head.

I look out the window and watch the orange and red skyline darken into a purple bruise as the sun dips below the Kansas horizon. The land is flat, and I imagine I can see all the way to the end of the earth.

The car slows and I sit up, gripping the seats in front of me for support.

I'm about to ask Dad why he's stopping in the middle of nowhere when I see the man with a guitar strapped to his back, a red bandana tied across his forehead, and a long gray ponytail tied low on his neck. He's holding out his thumb, his gray beard blowing on the breeze.

Willie Nelson, Country Music Singer/Song-writer

"We never stop for hitch-hikers," I say.

Dad shrugs. "We don't usually have room." It's true. This is our first move transporting two cars. "Besides," says Dad, "it's getting dark, and there's nothing for miles."

Dad pulls off the road and rolls down the front passenger window. I shrink into my seat as, I kid you not, Willie Nelson's long-lost cousin comes to the window.

Travel Log Note: If you've never heard of Willie Nelson, look him up. One of his most famous songs is "On the Road Again." It was something I hummed every time we got in the car as a kid.

My fifth grade teacher, Ms. Mitchell, taught us about subliminal messages in advertising—how cigarette companies use young, healthy models to make their product appealing. I'm convinced the country station Dad's been listening to has him feeling all warm and fuzzy, and the fact that the man resembles Willie doesn't hurt either.

Subliminal message aside, this is just one more case of Dad's "Superman Complex" flaring up again.

My dad's a big man. He was an ALL-WAC football player in college and stands at 6'5" with muscles that seem superhuman to a ten-year-old girl. He has a long and detailed history of assuming he is invincible: lifting heavy objects, swimming with sharks... He's the guy who intentionally doesn't lock his door because he's convinced he can "handle" any robber foolish enough to trespass.

I roll my eyes just thinking about the lecture Mom would give him for picking up the stranger.

My dad playing BYU football, 1982.

Travel Log Note: My dad is the definition of a giant teddy bear, but the guys I dated in high school and college never saw that side of him, for some reason. ☺

"Where are you headed?" Dad asks Willie with a grin.

"Wherever you're goin'." The old man's voice is gravel and grit.

Motioning back to me, Dad says, "You can put your guitar in back with Jenny."

My door is opened and I shrink back as the guitar, whose name happens to be Ole Bess, invades my precious space.

All I can think right now is how mad Mom is going to be when we pull up to the motel with Willie and Ole Bess, whose case smells like her owner: smoke, alcohol, and body odor. Dad cracks the windows just an inch or two.

"We're stopping tonight in Topeka," says Dad. He turns down the radio. "Is there somewhere in town you can stay?"

"Wherever you're staying works for me."

Dad pulls his eyes off the road, casting a double-take in the direction of our new travel companion. "But what is your final destination?" Dad asks again.

The man sits and rubs at his beard, as though he's never considered having a destination. "I suppose I'd like to see the ocean." (Reminder: we're still in Kansas.)

At his core, Dad is a military man. Though we are always on the road, our travels are calculated, strategic career moves. The idea that someone could live such a random existence frustrates the balance of my father's world. I can see it in the way Dad's hands flex on the steering wheel.

"We're moving to Florida to an Air Force base right next to Tampa Bay," I offer.

We are moving back to MacDill Air Force Base. We lived there two years ago. It's a nice place, with piers that stretch out over the ocean that attract pelicans the size of small children.

Dad frowns at me in the rearview mirror, as though I've said something wrong.

"Do you have family?" Dad asks.

"A couple of kids."

"Can I help you contact them?"

The old man shrugs. "Why?"

That silences my father.

Two hours later, when we finally pull into our motel parking lot, Dad shakes the man's hand, and I can tell he's slipped him some money, though I have no idea how much. "Happy trails."

I salute Willie and grab my pillow and backpack from the car. Dad leaves the windows cracked to air out the car overnight. When we finally get to our room, Mom whispers, "What took you so long?" The other kids are already asleep on one of the two beds. With distaste, I eye the sliver of space that I know is meant to be mine next to my wiggly little sister.

Mom hugs me, and by the way she sniffs my hair, I'm sure I smell just like Ole Bess.

Before she can ask where we've been, a guitar strums out the window of our room. Dad lifts the curtain enough for me to see Willie sitting on the asphalt, leaning against one of our car tires.

"I think he finally knows where he's going," I whisper to Dad, doing my best not to crack a smile at the thought of Willie tagging along for the rest of the trip.

Dad shuts the curtain. "Not in a million years."

Character Types

Imagine me as Gollum, rubbing my boney hands together with glee over this "precious" subject. I love discussing fictional characters because they have the power to make or break a story.

But before we can put the pedal to the metal discussing powerful characters, it is vital that you first have a basic understanding of the main types of characters used in storytelling. Consider this your vocabulary lesson for the day. ☺

Protagonist: The hero or heroine, the main character, the big cheese, the cat's meow, etc.
This is the character who faces the overwhelming conflict that must be resolved. There can be more than one protagonist in a story, but only if the characters share the "screen time" and narration follows each of their stories. If you know the story of Les Misérables, there are several big roles: Fantine, Èponine, Marius, Cosette, etc., but it is clear that Jean Valjean is the protagonist because the story opens and closes with him. Even though other characters are tested and developed, it is Valjean's metamorphosis that the story centers around.

Antagonist: The main villain, bad guy, the Dark Lord, supreme bad dude, Vader, etc.
This character represents the obstacle that the protagonist must overcome. There can be varying degrees of "bad guys" in your story. You'll often see

several evil characters doing the bidding of the main villain, but the antagonist is the primary force of opposition. In certain types of novels, the antagonist can be an animal, a natural element (such as a storm), or even a disease. In John Green's blisteringly brilliant novel *The Fault in Our Stars*, the antagonist is cancer.

Supporting (Secondary) Characters: Pretty self-explanatory.
These characters might be a sidekick, a best friend, a mentor, etc. Their job is to help or support the protagonist (Ron and Hermione) or antagonist (Lucius Malfoy and Bellatrix Lestrange) and move the plot forward.

Extras: Everyone else.
If your novel became a movie, this cast of characters would be "Bank Teller #1, Street Vendor #3, etc). Their names are often never used, and their purpose is to provide filler and setting to the story.

Who's Driving This Thing?

I can't remember the actual name of the old man who got in the car with my dad and me that night in Kansas, but I will never forget how frustrated Dad was that "Willie" was content to go wherever the wind blew him.

Fictional characters who wander through the pages of a story without true purpose are just as frustrating to readers. It is our job as writers to provide motivation for our characters. **The greater our character's motivation, the more exciting the story!**

If our characters love something or want something more than the air they breathe, not only are they more interesting, but also we as the author know exactly how to add conflict to the plot. Why? Because it is our job as writers to keep our characters from getting their heart's desire for as long as possible.

> **Travel Log Note**: We'll discuss creating gut-wrenching conflict for our protagonist in greater detail in Chapter 5.

You can strengthen your character's motivation by knowing their past.

Imagine if *you* are the main character of a story. Ask yourself what makes you who you are today. You wouldn't just appear on the page in the first chapter. Rather, you'd enter the story with a collection of life experiences that shape your thoughts and worldviews.

Here are a few examples:

- If you spent most of your life working in a butcher shop, you probably wouldn't have a problem with blood. You might also be good with a knife and have a general knowledge of anatomy.
- If you split your time between divorced parents and two separate homes, you might have experience with learning to adapt to new situations.
- If you are raised in a very religious home, your thoughts and actions might differ from someone raised to believe there isn't a god.
- If you ran away from an abusive home at a young age, didn't go to school, and lived on the street, you're probably very independent and street smart, but lack formal education. You might have developed the skills of a good thief that helped you survive. You're probably suffering from some emotional damage as well and are slow to trust others.

Do you see how characters can develop right before your eyes just by creating a past for them?

If you already know your character's personality, take a moment to decide how they came to be the way they are. If they're angry at the world, figure out why. If they have a strong moral conscience, create a reason. If they love something or someone, justify it. Be sure to keep the character's actions in line with their personality. This means a goody-two-shoes probably won't swear or break rules, or a really well-educated person won't speak with bad grammar, etc.

Once you've decided on your character's history or backstory, make sure your character's actions, thoughts, and dialogue reflect that history. Keep in mind: it is important that you don't dump all of your character's history into the first page or even the first chapter of a novel. In fact, that is exactly what you *don't* want to do. Rather, treat your character's history like a secret that you, the author, get to divulge only when the timing is right. Allow your reader to wonder why your character behaves the way they do. Your character should be a mystery that the reader is dying to solve.

You will eventually want your reader to know your character's secrets, but you'll do it in a way that resembles Hansel and Gretel leaving a trail of breadcrumbs. Here a little, there a little, teasing the reader with morsels of yummy information they've been dying to gobble up.

Essential Questions Your Characters Must Answer

Building our main character's past is the first, and perhaps most, important step to knowing our characters.

But it is definitely not the only step.

If you sense another list coming on, prepare to be right! If we expect our readers to see our characters as real, breathing people, we definitely need to know them on that level.

Here is my list of essential questions you must be able to answer about both your protagonist AND your antagonist before you can effectively write them. It doesn't hurt to also know some of the answers for your secondary characters as well.

1. What is their defining moment?

This is not a moment that takes place in your story. Rather, it is a moment that defines your character before the novel even begins. This moment might be the day your character's mom left, the day they fell out of a tree and became a quadriplegic, the day they joined the circus, the day they stood up to a bully, etc.

Harry Potter's defining moment was not the day he received his letter to Hogwarts; it was the day he received his scar.

Basically, this is just one more way to help you discover your character's past and motivation.

2. What is your character's greatest weakness?

Good characters have weaknesses. The best characters have one monster weakness that serves as their kryptonite, their Achilles' heel. Writers, who tend to be a bit dramatic, call this weakness the "fatal flaw." I've never loved that label, mostly because unless you're writing a Greek tragedy, the flaw can't be totally fatal because the character should come out conqueror in the end.

> **Travel Log Note**: My fatal flaw is junior mints. I'm sure when they determine my cause of death, the doctor will shake her head in regret and say, "It was touch and go there for a while, but in the end, the overdose got the best of her."

I once heard a story about hunters in Africa trying to catch and transport a troop of monkeys. Instead of setting netted traps or trying to shoot and tranquilize the monkeys out of the trees, the trappers simply placed small wooden boxes filled with nuts on the forest floor with holes just large enough for the monkey to get its hand through. The monkeys would reach in and grab a handful of nuts, but they couldn't pull their hand out of the small hole without letting go of the nuts.

When the trappers came, the monkeys screamed in panic at the approaching men, but they couldn't run away because they were not willing to drop the nuts and free their hand.

Your character's greatest weakness needs to be the nut your character struggles to release. Something they feel powerless to defeat but must overcome if they hope to survive the main conflict of the story. It's best if this weakness causes your character to fail on minor levels throughout the story and *almost* destroys them in the climax.

The more you develop this weakness throughout the story, the greater the payoff when your character triumphs over it.

3. What do they want most in life?

We've spent quite a bit of time addressing this question already in this chapter, but I will reiterate that knowing our character's motivations and goals is a huge pillar to your plot and cannot be undervalued.

Be sure to take the time to understand what your antagonist desires most, and the *why* behind that desire. Simply stating that they are power hungry and want to rule the world is not good enough. No evil person sets out to do horrible things just for the sake of being evil. Build up your antagonist's history. Create reasons for them to justify their desires. See the situation through their eyes. Most villains would never guess they are a villain. Evil is always in the eye of the beholder.

4.   What do people assume about your character that is not true?
Have you ever felt as though no one really understands you? Of course you have. This is because you are the only person with full knowledge of your thoughts, your history, actions, motives, etc. We all have a strong desire for justice to prevail, and we all know what it's like to be misunderstood.

Not only is having your character misunderstood by others relatable to the reader, it is also a great way to add tension. Put yourself in the shoes of other characters in the story and see how they would perceive your character.

Your character might have a reputation for disrespecting a teacher by sleeping through class. But what if no one at school realizes he works graveyard shifts in the shipyard because his dad died last year and his family needs the money.

Readers will feel that injustice. In fact, they will devour pages to see the misunderstanding resolved and justice restored. Any time you can create a reason for readers to cheer on your main character, you're doing something right!

5.   What does your character assume that is not true?
This question turns that last question on its head and is another great way to add internal conflict to a story.

It is so important that we avoid making our characters too perfect. Perfection is boring and not at all relatable to the reader, so go ahead and allow your character to carry around some false beliefs.

Perhaps your character (due to one bad experience) has labeled an entire race or class of people as evil. Maybe she assumes that she will never have the talent to be a prima ballerina. Perhaps he falsely believes that fighting is the only way to find peace, or that conventional medicine can solve a magical disease that is killing his mother.

Adding these false assumptions can be a great way to show growth in a character over the course of a story. Allow your character to overcome prejudice, self-doubt, or a false sense of how they world operates.

We want our characters to be dynamic, and the definition of dynamic is *change*. If your character already knows everything they need to know or has everything they want, how can we show that they've developed into something *more* over the course of the story?

6.   What is your main character's stereotype?

Yes, I'm talking about the convention stereotypes you might hear in the halls of any high school across the United States—jock, prep, nerd, goth, geek, drama, band, mean girl, popular, druggy, etc. If you write fantasy, you might be thinking, "My story doesn't even take place in our world, let alone a high school!" But I promise this question still applies.

Pretend that your main character attends your school. With which crowd would they associate? Ask yourself why. You may discover some cool new insights about your character, but mostly we need to know their stereotype because we need to know how we're going to break it. (See next question.)

7.   How do they break their stereotype?

Great characters have the ability to surprise us. They go from being okay to fascinating and obsession-worthy by breaking conventional molds. Here's an example to help illustrate my point:

Character #1: *Brian scores three touchdowns in the big homecoming game. After the game he hits the showers then attends the homecoming celebration with his friends.*

Character #2: *Brian scores three touchdowns in the big homecoming game. After the game he hits the showers, then sneaks into the city to perform slam poetry.*

Which character is more interesting to you? Which character has you asking questions?

Our brains are fascinating computers that love to label, compare, contrast, and organize information. Readers subconsciously slap tags on characters all the time. When we set up the reader to believe our character fits a certain mold, and then we break that stereotype, our reader's brain will flag this as interesting and unique. If we hadn't established Brian's stereotype as a jock beforehand, the slam poetry wouldn't be nearly so cool. It is the mold-breaking that we love.

Other examples of broken stereotypes:
- The class clown who's terrified of public speaking.
- The dancer who works as a mechanic.
- The banker who doesn't manage his own money well.
- The chemist who doubles as a nightclub bouncer on the weekends.
- The thief who robs from the rich to feed the poor. (Sound familiar?)

When executed well, breaking stereotypes breathes life and a sense of unpredictability into our characters. It'll have your reader leaning forward, excited to see what you'll do next to surprise them.

Finding a Character's Voice

In the publishing world, the term "voice" refers to the tone of the narration of the story.

Let's pretend the book you're writing follows the story of a boy named Felix. Whether you are writing in first or third person, Felix's voice should come through in the narration. The sentences and word choice should *sound* as though Felix is telling the story.

Voice should reflect age, life experience, and the character's personality. If Felix is a sixteen-year-old country boy who comes to the city for the first time, he will describe a scene very differently than a cab driver from New York City. Felix would take notice of how loud the city is, of the number of people walking in every direction, of the diversity. These are things that to a New York City native would seem commonplace. We can tell a lot about a character by knowing what surprises them… and what doesn't.

Felix is the storyteller. You (the author) are not. It is your job to get out of Felix's way and let him tell his own story. Yes, I know this all sounds rather strange, but it makes a huge difference to the reader.

Too often, writers do not spend time developing their protagonist's voice before writing. One of the most effective ways I've learned to discover the voice of a character is by journaling from their point of view. I see it almost as a get-to-know-you session… as though my protagonist walks into my living room, sits on my couch and tells me who they are, what they love, their history, etc.

I treat this journaling as a "free write" or brainstorming session. I write as much as I can without over-thinking grammar, sentence structure, etc. Nothing from the free write is meant to go directly into your book. It only serves the purpose of discovery.

Here is a small segment of a character journal I wrote when I was trying to discover the voice of Fina Perona. She is the protagonist in the young adult fantasy novel I'm currently writing. Even though the book is written in third person, when I journal a character to discover their voice, I always write in first person, allowing me to get right inside the character's head.

FINA PERONA JOURNAL

My name is Fina Perona and I don't like you. There. I've said it. Now, if I've played my cards right, you will leave me alone. That's all a person like me can ask for—to be left alone. I prefer that to quiet fear or indifference.

I have a scar on my arm. Some call it the Mark of the Serpent. I don't know if they're right. Believe them if you like. It makes no difference to me. Remember? I don't care about you.

So please, whatever you do, don't send your pity my way. I'd rather chew on wet seaweed than your pity, thank you very much. I'm strong enough without your acceptance.

I live in a small fishing village in Vino Antico. We are famous for tart white wine that nicely compliments our fish, as well as our hankering for superstition. My favorite color is red. Why? Because my father used to always compliment the red ribbons Mama tied in my hair. He'd say it matched my lips and kiss my cheeks before leaving to work in our family vineyard. But red is also the color of anger, blood, and fear. I hate, HATE the sight of blood. It makes me think of the worst day of my life. The day I stopped being an innocent girl who lived on a small oceanside vineyard, and became a monster.

Father Thomas tells me that it isn't true. That the mark on my arm is just a scar from a bad accident. He says God wouldn't mark an innocent child, but sometimes I don't believe him. Sometimes believing in the curse is easier than accepting the fact that people hate me for nothing . . .

That is, if I cared, of course.

Which I don't.

I learn a great deal about my characters through these journal sessions.

When I wrote this journal, I knew nothing of Vino Antico, Father Thomas, Fina's love of the color red, etc. These ideas just sprang into my mind as I was free writing.

Do you notice how journaling demands characterization? It forces the writer to take on the role of the character—to breathe life, history, and purpose into that character until they become, for us, a real person. Journaling in this way is very similar to the task actors have of taking on a role and getting inside their character's head in a way that feels like they become the character.

Once you learn how to create three-dimensional characters, you'll find that many of the other elements of novel writing, such as plot, tension, etc., naturally fall into place. The best part of all: creating dynamic characters is one of the most entertaining steps in the writing process. Use your imagination. Have fun! More than anything else, make certain your characters are going places—that they have goals and dreams. Without motivation, all you'll have is a wandering Willie Nelson wanna-be with bad body odor.

Hit the Road: Characterization Writing Prompt

Part One: Answer the seven questions listed in this chapter from your character's point of view.

1. What is your character's defining moment?
2. What is your character's greatest weakness?
3. What does your character want most in life?
4. What do people assume about your character that is not true?
5. What does your character assume that is not true?
6. What is your character's stereotype?
7. How does your character break it?

Part Two: Write a journal entry in the voice and character of your protagonist *and* your antagonist. Be sure to include as much personality as possible in each entry.

3

World Building in Progress: Proceed with Caution

"Mom, the pelicans! Who will save the pelicans?" I shout over the roaring wind and the worried cries of my seven-year-old little sister.

It was 5:00 p.m. on August 24, 1992, when the order to evacuate came. Like the giant in Jack's beanstalk, Hurricane Andrew has stomped through the Bahamas and the islands off the southern tip of Florida and is now headed toward our home on MacDill Air Force Base at frightening speed. The fearsome wind and rain rattling the windows seems to cry, "Fee-fi-fo-fum."

I don't even like pelicans.

Mom and I used to walk across the street to the pier with Whitney in the stroller and Josh running around looking for rocks to throw. My older brother was always throwing rocks. We'd feed

NASA view of hurricanes

the massive birds as they sat on their weathered, wooden thrones. It was all fun and games until the day an angry bird extended its long, go-go-gadget neck and almost took my little fingers along with the bread.

Now white waves crash over the pier and the birds' kingly perches sit abandoned, just like our home will be in a matter of minutes.

Mom pulls the last of the photo albums down from the bookshelf and jams it into a laundry basket filled with a few other sentimental items that have made the hasty cut. "Everyone in the car!" she orders, as though she, and not my father, has the military background.

I tuck my pillow and Rainbow Brite doll close to my chest and pile into the station wagon with my brother and sister.

The moment we leave the garage, I'm sure we're not going to make it to our friend's home a few miles inland. Josh hoots with excitement as an especially large gust of wind rocks our car. Mom's hands tighten on the wheel. Palm tree branches line the road and roofing shingles fly across our windshield.

Hurricane Andrew devastation

Mom's tough, but I wish Dad were here to drive. If nothing else, his extra weight might keep the car from blowing away.

But the government thinks it needs Dad more than we do. He and the rest of the F-16 pilots have orders to get the expensive jets safely away from the coast and Hurricane Andrew's clutches.

Not far from our house and the pier, a water spout drags the ocean up into a cyclone of grayish blue, and all I can do is press my hand to the car window and mutter, "Fee-fi-fo-fum" under my breath over and over.

In a Perfect World...

World building is without a doubt one of the most important decisions writers make when approaching a work of fiction. It can also be one of the most exciting aspects of writing, especially within sci-fi/fantasy genres. Great world builders understand that setting can act a little like a secondary character in your story and should serve the plot.

Setting acting as a character? It seems crazy, right? It means that professional writers consider character and conflict as they decide on a setting/world.

Had the vignette at the beginning of the chapter been a work of fiction, I might have selected a setting that placed the characters in even greater danger, with greater stakes. Perhaps at a time in history without big government relief efforts, or in a world where growing crops was vital to my family's survival and fatal storms result in financial ruin for the family. Perhaps I would have inserted an ailing grandparent unable to travel because our village didn't have serviceable roads and we had to hike over a mountain to safety.

Do you notice how a world/setting can be bent to add tension to a story?

Next, I'd consider how I could tweak the setting to highlight the strengths and/or weaknesses of the main character. A flash flood might provide the perfect opportunity to show a character's heroic nature or, by contrast, a fear of water and inability to swim. Major calamity can show a character's resourcefulness as well as demonstrate what the character values above all else.

Creating a Sense of Wonder

I have a slightly embarrassing confession to make...

I cry every time I walk into Disneyland. Not a weeping, flailing, ugly cry, just a few alligator tears of joy. I hear the sounds of a brass band playing, inhale the smell of buttery popcorn and churros, and delight in the green animal topiaries and elaborate flowerbeds surrounding me. The columns of old-fashioned buildings act like the portal of a time machine, and with every step closer to the heart of the park, I leave my regular, boring life behind and escape into Walt's magic.

I have a similar tear-inducing reaction every time I launch a boat at Lake Powell in Bullfrog, Utah. The sight of the towering red rock cliffs coupled with the knowledge that I'm surrounded by family, water, and sunshine transport me to my proverbial happy place.

Both places are extremely different. One offers solitude and nature and the other offers fantasy and whimsy, but one key element unites these examples of setting in my mind: transportation.

I know this book is all about road trip references, but I'm not talking about *that* kind of transportation. I refer instead to the kind of experience that plucks us out of our normal, everyday lives and plants us in another time, another place.

From realistic fiction to high fantasy, any type of setting can transport a reader so long as the writer infuses *originality* and—just as in Walt's Disneyland—*little nuggets of details.*

Let's challenge my proposed theory.

Say we want to write a book set in present-day St. Louis. Perhaps most of the scenes from the story take place inside a high school. This has the train-wreck potential to be an extremely mundane setting, right? How can we make this pedestrian setting original?

Well, what if the school is located in a reclaimed sweat factory? What if the community believes it might be haunted by the ghosts of children who died working there? What if the building is riddled with old metal chutes (think slides) that have been boarded up and are discovered over the course of the book?

> **Travel Log Note**: Notice that crazy-awesome ideas come from "What If" questions!

Can you see how using a typical high school feels a little like a missed opportunity? Now let's consider a few little nuggets of detail that might breathe life into our factory-turned-school:

- Original brickwork with faded initials carved from a child long ago

- Bare-bulb light fixtures that flicker
- Spiral iron staircases meant to save space that snag the clothing of passersby
- Dormant smoke stacks that still seem to give off smoke
- A curious draft down a central hallway
- Original lockers used by sweat factory employees

Travel Log Note: We will be digging deeper into descriptive detail in Chapter 7.

Even if our story does not delve into paranormal ghosts, this setting can provide a unique, powerful framework that influences the mood and overall "transportation factor" of the book.

Introducing Readers to Your World

I am currently working on a book set in the American colonies during the Revolutionary War. Historical fiction is like writing fantasy but with something I like to call "world building accountability." When plotting this novel, I wanted an excuse to show the world without jamming too much description down the reader's throat in the first chapter.

This can be a tricky balance in which less is usually more.

The story opens with a fire in British-occupied Long Island in September of 1776. Starting with the fire was a strategic decision because it placed my characters in an active environment where I could show off my world without boring my readers to tears by rambling off a list of sights. Because the fire is fundamental to the plot, I can delve into architecture as buildings burn and show insights into culture, technology (or lack thereof), fashion, geography, etc., all while introducing the main characters and conflicts of the story. The fire also provides a sense of destruction and loss—a mood I wanted the readers to feel to help them understand the desperation of the early American patriots.

As you consider your approach to world building and your opening scene, I recommend challenging the logical first idea that comes into your mind. Usually, with a little flexing of the imagination, you can make your world just a little more unique.

Ask yourself the questions:

- Can I be more original? (Remember your "what if" questions!)
- Am I including those little nuggets of detail that will transport my reader?
- Does the opening scene give readers a good introduction to the world without slowing down the story?

Remember, you only get to make a first impression once. Pack the biggest punch you can!

Requirements for a Civilization

How do authors such as J. K. Rowling, J. R. R. Tolkien, and Brandon Sanderson develop worlds that feel so real they seem to blur the lines between fiction and reality?

Orson Scott Card said, "To be a good world builder, you have to know how the world works."

As a historian, I've attended countless lectures on the foundations of civilization and can tell you there's a lot more to creating an authentic civilization than just incorporating a cool magic system or mythical creatures.

I'll spare you the college tuition fees and boil world building down into six vital areas.

1.   How was your world created?

Does your story take place on earth? If the answer is "Yes!" then this question won't require much reflection. If the answer is "No" or "I never thought about it," then you have a few things to consider.

Even if you have no intention of going into any detail about the geological history of your world, knowing the answer to this question can help you add depth to your plot.

Consider the sky.

The sun, moon, and stars have always been so important to mankind. On a surface level, they offer light and warmth, impact ocean currents, and really make life possible on earth. On a cultural level, they determine clothing, influence artists, assist with navigation, and can even provide the energy to power buildings.

What do your characters see when they look up into the sky? How does what they see effect their lives? There is nothing wrong with patterning your fictitious world after our own, but make sure that you're not missing out on interesting, creative ways to make your setting unique.

Are there any geological wonders or scientific rules that differ from Earth's? Perhaps in your world the rules of gravity change the closer you get to the north and south poles. Perhaps your world is found on a planet that rotates on its axis at twice the speed of earth, causing ocean currents to travel in only one direction. Perhaps your ozone is deteriorating, causing sun flares or ether storms. Or perhaps your world doesn't have an axis at all, so some lands are perpetually cold while others are perpetually warm. The possibilities are endless!

2.   What is the geography of the world?

Mountains, desert, ocean, forest… all can be wonderful places to set a story, but be careful to consider the benefits and weaknesses of any given setting. For a world to feel believable, the geography should provide what the characters inhabiting the story need to survive. For humans or humanoids, that means shelter, food, and water.

Water is a huge resource for humans, animals, and plants. Ask yourself how your characters get their drinking water. How do they irrigate their crops? You may be writing a story that has absolutely nothing to do with farming or feasting, but knowing the answers to these questions is extremely important.

There is nothing worse then a story written about a desert people with no regard to water shortages and who feast on water-loving crops. Unless you make a really big deal about some underground water oasis, it's too improbable to feel authentic to your reader.

Another item to consider about geography is a society's ability to defend itself. Even if your story has nothing to do with war or conquest, it is narrow-minded to assume that the people who founded your village/city/country would not have strategically located its heart in a defensible position. Large bodies of water, mountain ranges, islands, high ground, wetlands—all provide some kind of defensive advantage.

3. What plants and animals can be found in your world?

Have you ever noticed that almost all fantasy worlds include horses? The mind's capacity for creativity is limitless, yet seldom do writers veer from this method of transportation in the fantasy genre. One great exception to this unwritten rule is found in the epic story *Children of Blood and Bone* by Tomi Adeyemi. In place of horses, creatures that resemble giant jungle cats called leopanaires, lionaires, and panthanaires carry the characters where they need to go. The author wanted to give a nod to her Western African heritage, and the result was creative genius.

Besides transportation, consider the by-products of animals that might influence the food and clothing of the inhabitance of your world.

Also ask what types of vegetation can be found in your world. If your story is modeled after a climate from this world, make sure that you're not missing subtle opportunities to add to or change the flora. Clothing dyes, medicines, architecture, weaponry, woven goods, and—the most obvious—FOOD all say something about what is grown.

Consider the climate. Staple crops like wheat, corn, and barley grow best in locations that experience four seasons, giving the fields a time to sleep through winter, while crops like rice, bananas, and sugar cane grow best in wet climates.

You may be thinking, *I don't need to know these kind of details*, but if characters plan to eat anything—or wear anything, for that matter—over the course of your story, knowing a little about the crops and by-products of animals in your world will go a long way to making everything feel authentic.

4. What type of economy exists in your world?

Within a certain geographical location, like a single town or even a county or state, it is unlikely that *all* commodities can be produced there. Unless your world consists of one group of people who all live in the same sphere of influence and never have any exposure to people from other regions of your world, the question of trade and transportation is vital.

Allow me to put on my historian hat for a second.

From roughly 200 BCE to 200 CE, traders from the East shipped spices such as "black gold" or pepper, silks, precious stones, furs, technology, and more using a trade route called the Silk Road that connected Asia to Europe. The Silk Road inspired the building of the Great Wall of China and fostered the development of major civilizations such as Japan, India, Iran, and Korea.

But was it just a trade route?

What many don't realize is that the two largest commodities exchanged on this route were ideas (think Renaissance) and disease (plague).

I could go on an on about the Silk Road and the connections built between countries by trade, but I'll boil it all down to this one point: silks from China and spices from India were desirable in Europe because they were hard to find. Knowing what your world/society lacks will help you develop depth to the economics of world building and depth to your plot.

5. What do the people of your world value and believe?

Your reader can learn a lot about your world by understanding what the people value. This can sometimes be manifested in an organized religion or belief system. If you have no interest in developing an intricate religion into your story, that's definitely okay. However, it is important to consider including some kind of moral code or standard of ethics. By doing so you have the opportunity to show your reader what is valued.

> **Travel Log Note**: Did you know that in Switzerland you're not allowed to flush the toilet after 10 p.m.? It's considered noise pollution. This random law shows that peaceful evenings are highly valued in their culture.

Here are some good questions to consider while developing a cultural belief system or religion:

a) What belief or beliefs are core to the characters' religion(s)/culture?

b) How did the belief develop and spread over time?

c) What does the afterlife look like? Does the culture have a story explaining the creation of the world?

d) How organized is the belief system/religion? Does it rely on one charismatic leader or group of leaders?

e) Do geography and economy affect the belief system(s)?

f) Does the culture have rituals that coincide with beliefs?

In my Nameless trilogy, each of the clans valued very different things (power, honesty, intellect, trade) and each had its own religious customs and belief system. While writing the books, I enjoyed developing rituals that centered around what each clan valued. For example, in the Ram Clan, a man's shield was a symbol of honor and pride. Here is a passage from *Nameless* that illustrates the engagement ceremony between a man and a woman in the Ram Clan:

Eva stepped inside the square of tables where Taurus waited with a smile too large for his face. He handed Eva a wand of sage and placed his round shield at her feet. She stepped up to the altar, twisting the bundle of herbs in her hands.

Eva's whisper sent a wave of chills up Gryphon's back.

"I claim your shield as my shield. May it protect our family and always bring you home." She dropped the sage into the fire. It hissed and cracked, causing fragrant clouds of smoke to rise from the flame and waft over the group.

Taurus drew his knife. He stepped closer to Eva and gathered her hair in his fist. "I claim your beauty and your womb. May our family bring honor to the Ram."

Rather barbaric, isn't it? But the ritual demonstrates so much about what is valued and important in Ram culture—honor, strength, clan unity—creating a sense of depth that allows readers to fall headfirst into the world.

6. How is power distributed and organized?

This is another area in which my inner historian is itching to explode onto the page, but I will refrain from ranting on the subject of government and politics. I'll simply say that mankind, since the Neolithic era of hunters and gatherers, has relied on systems of government to keep order and peace. Sometimes that system is obtained through violence. Other systems are created through debate and peaceful agreements.

It is important to know and understand how the power in your world is distributed in your society. Just to get your creative juices flowing, here are some examples of governments from which to draw inspiration:

Forms of Government	Definition	Example
Autocracy	A country or nation that is governed by a single person with unlimited power.	**Theocracy**: The Vatican is ruled by the Pope. **Absolute Monarchy**: Henry VIII in England **Dictatorship**: Adolf Hitler in Germany in WWII
Oligarchy	The rule of a few. (Power typically comes from wealth, power, or social status)	**Ancient Greek city-states** **Council of Elders**: Some Native American tribes and the people of Turkmenistan
Democracy	The rule of many.	**Democratic Republic**: The United States **Constitutional Monarchy**: Present-day Great Britain **Parliament**: The New Republic in *Star Wars* ☺

Consider the impact government has on the plot on and main character(s). If that impact is very little, your knowledge of politics and power in government doesn't need to be as extensive. But knowing at least the basic structure of government—particularly who has power and how that power is used—will add life to your world and may influence your plot.

Ask these questions as you consider politics and the distribution of power in your world:

a) How do the people of your world respond to the government? Do they support those in power? Oppose them? Are they indifferent?
b) What was life like before the government?
c) To whom are those in power accountable?
d) Are there any laws or regulations that impact your main character and/or plot?

Remember that almost every aspect of life can be affected by government, including laws, civil rights, protection from crime, taxes, and trade of economic goods. Have fun with this! Use "What if" questions to explore cool new angles to develop your story.

Magic Systems and Staying in Your Own Lane

Readers devour tales of magic and the supernatural, but incorporating a magic system into your story can be a lot like switching lanes in rush hour traffic.

> **Travel Log Note**: This author would like to credit Boston, MA, for having the craziest rush hour drivers in the country. Give it up for Bean Town!

There are really two types of magic systems that can help determine how much your story relies on magic.

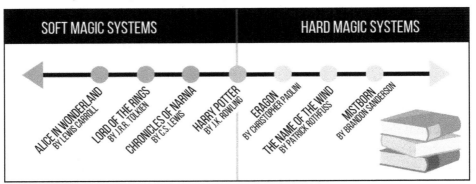

Soft Magic Systems & Hard Magic Systems

In *soft magic systems* the reader knows very little of how the magic works. This is also sometimes referred to as "unlimited magic" because the magic is unexplained and therefore the reader isn't certain just how much the "wand waver" can accomplish. This type of system is a favorite for stories that include magical creatures, wizards, and fairy tales.

Soft magic systems are fantastic at creating a sense of wonder for the reader. Because the restrictions of the magic are unexplained, there is also an element of unpredictability that can be exciting for readers and provide an excellent opportunity for the writer to get creative with plot and world building.

There are some disadvantages to writing soft magic systems though, and it's important to decide just how large a role you want the magic to play in your plot.

Often in soft magic systems the main characters—whose perspective we follow in the narration—don't wield magic themselves, or if they do, they are one of many and the magic is portrayed as commonplace.

This is the case because the solution to the main conflict in soft magic systems should come not by magic but instead by the main characters' heroic actions. The reader must feel that the main conflict has been resolved by means of great sacrifice, otherwise the victory feels cheap.

Good examples of a soft system can be found in Tolkien's Lord of the Rings series and *The Hobbit*. The magic of Middle Earth is never explained in much detail. The wizard Gandalf simply walks into the story with set powers that aren't defined for the reader. Because the story is told through the eyes of the hobbits, we don't know Gandalf's limitations or even what he had to do to obtain his power. We just know that he's powerful, that his power has limits, and that he occasionally uses that power to get the hobbits out of bad situations. In these books, it is often the character's race that delineates his or her power. Elves can live forever because they are elves, etc.

In Lord of the Rings, the act of disposing of the ring would not be nearly so heroic if Gandalf magically transported them where they needed to go. Tolkien split up the fellowship of the ring so that Frodo's journey would feel genuine and hard-earned, while preserving the beautiful magic-infused world of Middle Earth.

Other good examples of soft magic systems include *Alice in Wonderland* and the Chronicles of Narnia.

In *hard magic systems* the reader learns a great deal about how the magic works over the course of the book. Hard systems are notorious for the reader getting to learn about the magic system with the main character. There are usually strict limitations to power and a high cost for using the magic. These systems depend on the magic to help solve the main conflict of the story.

I consider Brandon Sanderson the master of hard magic systems. When I first read his Mistborn series, it changed the way I looked at magic. In fact, if you really want to dig deeper into learning about magic systems, I recommend you look up "Sanderson's Laws of Magic."

Christopher Paolini's novel *Eragon* is another good example of a hard magic system. We see the hero as a farm boy living a humble life without magic and then get to follow him through the process of learning to call magic forth. To use magic, he uses the resources around him—pulling water from the ground for drinking, taking heat from living things to form fire, etc. He must know the appropriate words to cast spells and the magic requires the sacrifice of his own strength.

> **Travel Log Note**: I would add that *Eragon* does have elements of soft magic because of the dragon Saphira. She occasionally wields powers even she doesn't understand.

Again, it's important to decide just how large a role you want the magic to play in your plot when you're deciding on your magic system.

Hit the Road: World Building Writing Prompt

Part One: Examine your setting. Is there a way you can make it more original? What details can you include that will *transport* your reader into your imaginary world?

Part Two: Answer the following six questions to better understand you imaginary world.

1. How was your world created?
2. What is the geography of the world?
3. What plants and animals can be found in your world?
4. What types of trade exist in your world and how are they transported?
5. What do the people of your world value and believe?
6. How is power distributed and organized?
7. If your world has a magic system, would a soft or hard system be more appropriate? Why?

4

Many Roads to One Destination

Did you know there are two different access roads to the Grand Canyon? Me neither...

The van is loaded with luggage, snacks, and authors. Teen Author Boot Camp—a teen writers conference I help organize in Utah—is complete. All that remains is the drive to show some of our out-of-state guests to a few of southern Utah's historical and geological gems before they travel home.

Authors Julie Reece, Leigh Statham, Amy Beatty, and editor/publisher Emma Nelson trust me with this task, and I'm determined to show them a good time.

We arrive in Kanab and spend our first day exploring the Little Hollywood Museum and a sand cave filled with a rainbow of colors. The day ends with a good dinner and delightful writing critique session. I can hardly sleep, I'm so excited for what we have planned for tomorrow.

"You're going to want a big breakfast, ladies. Plan on hiking!" I say, pulling open the fridge the next morning. I then proceed to rattle off a few of the hiking options and a list of all of the virtues of the majestic Grand Canyon. I'm good at sounding like I know what I'm talking about, even though I've only been to the legendary canyon one other time... several years ago...when coming home from a trip to Flagstaff, Arizona.

Travel Log Note: Did you know you can see the Grand Canyon from outer space? Seriously cool.

We load into the van, buckle up, and I drive us down the US 89 to show

Grand Canyon Road Closed Sign

these women one of the Seven Wonders of the Natural World.

"I'm so excited!" Julie literally bounces in the front seat. The Georgia author has never been this far west. This will be the highlight of her trip and unlike anything she's ever seen—a big red check off her proverbial bucket list. I'm glad I get to be the one to help her fulfill this dream.

I'm practically bouncing myself—until I see the sign that kills all of my plans for the day.

So apparently you can access the North Rim of the Grand Canyon from the once famous "Little Hollywood" town of Kanab, Utah, or you can ac-cess the South Rim via a tiny Arizona resort town called Tusayan. The road that takes you to the South Rim through Arizona is open year-round. The road to the North Rim is closed from November to March.

I probably should have checked on that before we made plans. Thankfully, we found an abandoned saloon in

Left to Right: Julie Reece, Emma Nelson, Amy Beatty, Leigh Statham, Jennifer Jenkins

Kanab's Little Hollywood Museum to drown our sorrows of missing the Grand Canyon.

You might approach a piece of writing like I did my little road trip to the North Rim. You know you want to get to a pre-determined destination in your plot, but you don't take the time to research the road. Your writing journey may eventually lead you to the place you had envisioned, but it comes with many detours, throw-away chapters, edits, and frustration. I'm convinced that the first step to avoiding these problems is identifying what kind of writer you are…

Plotting vs. Pantsing
(not that kind of pantsing!)

I think we all understand the basic idea of plotting, but pantsing? Yes, you did read that right. A "pantser" is a term authors use to represent someone who "writes by the seat of their pants." These types of writers are also known as discovery writers.

Not every writer is strictly either a plotter or a pantser. There is a lot of gray area between the two extremes. By identifying your style and approach to writing, you can go into a project prepared to handle the pros and cons of each approach.

Plotting: No GPS? No Problem

Strict pantsers work off of a primary source of inspiration and use that spark to fill the pages of a full novel. They may be inspired by a cool plot concept, an idea for a new character, or even a setting—be it real or imagined. Whatever the source, they use that inspiration as a springboard to start writing. They don't take the time to flesh out all of the characters or plot points, instead letting the artistic inspiration of the piece guide them through their writing journey.

I personally love pantsing and have written more than one book this way. I find that my best ideas come when my imagination is free of boundaries. I'm often surprised by the direction the story takes. Here's the catch: I've found that as my knowledge of story structure grows over the years, my ability to "pants" increases.

In this chapter, we will go over all of the major "pit stops" of story structure. Once you have a firm grasp of all of the elements of story, we can then discuss a few plotting techniques for plotters, pantsers, and those who find themselves somewhere in-between.

Plotting Pit Stops

Whether you prefer "pantsing" or heavy plotting, writing is a journey and there's more than one way to reach your destination. Before you start writing, here are a few "pit stops" or vital moments I strongly encourage you to consider that will help you enjoy the drive. These pit stops are checkpoints that will keep the reader engaged and further the plot.

Plotting Pit Stop #1
The Starting Line

Beginnings are actually quite tricky. They provide the reader with the very first glimpse into your world and the minds of your characters. And in today's society, if you don't learn how to grab the interest of the reader early, there is a very real possibility they'll give up on the story after the first chapter.

I want you to imagine that you're fishing. It's a nice, crisp autumn morning. The leaves are showing off a burst of colors, warning that winter is on the way. Your tackle box knocks against your knee as you hike down the steep trail to the local pond. The bugs are out. The fish are jumping for their morning meal. You settle onto a thick tuft of grass and it's time to bait your hooks.

Notice I didn't say "hook."

Your fishing line is unique because it has not one, not two, but many hooks, and you plan to bait them all before casting that pole into the water.

Just like our imaginary fishing pole, your first chapter can and should have many hooks to properly engage your reader.

Hook #1: The First Line

The first line of a story is a reader's first impression and shouldn't be handled lightly. Your first line should immediately snag the reader's attention—getting them curious enough to continue turning pages.

You can make your reader curious in several ways, be it a false or ironic statement, a shocking or curious action, or a very carefully crafted description. Whether you begin with action, dialogue, or description, the key element of that first line is to get your reader to ask themselves a simple question: Why?

Here is an example of a first line hook using internal dialogue:

"Blue Sargent had forgotten how many times she'd been told that she would kill her true love." —*The Raven Boys* by Maggie Stiefvater

I love this example because it inspires so many questions! Who would tell Blue such a thing? How would they know? Does she believe them? Will she actually kill her true love? Do people have psychic abilities in this book?

This example is extra amazing because it hints at what the reader assumes might be the main conflict of the story by promising a star-crossed love story.

Here is another example of a great first line hook, this time using description:

"I stare down at my shoes, watching as a fine layer of ash settles on the worn leather. This is where the bed I shared with my sister, Prim, stood." —*Mockingjay* by Suzanne Collins

This is a great first line (okay, two lines) because it sets a mood for the story, hints at heavy backstory, and has us asking questions such as why is there ash in the air? What is burning? Who set the fire? What happened to her sister?

This final example is a great example of an action hook using dialogue.

"I've confessed to everything and I'd like to be hanged. Now, if you please." —*Chime* by Franny Billingsley.

Holy questions, Batman! What has she confessed? Does she have a desire to die? Is she, perhaps, trying to cover for someone? Why hanging? Is this historical? Why is she so calm?

The questions are endless, making for a powerful hook.

Hook #2: Characterization

Just as with the first line hook, a character hook only works if a protagonist's introduction has us asking questions. Characters who break stereotype are sure to pique the interest of the reader. It is our job to place our characters in a scene that will bring out the unique attributes of the character that will ignite curiosity in your reader.

From the very beginning of the story we should be asking the question WHY?

Why are they running from the police?

Why is the small kid picking a fight she knows she will lose?

Why is he diving for food in a dumpster while wearing a gold watch?

Why is he smiling while that gun is pointed at his head?

Why is she being rude to the man who just helped her down from that horse?

Why is the likeable man robbing a bank?

In all of these "why" questions, the character is taking a conventional response or behavior and turning it on its head, making the reader curious. Showcasing the unexpected is a perfect way to hook a reader using characterization.

Hook #3: Conflict

Humans are hardwired to problem solve. It's a survival skill we all possess. The moment we see a problem or conflict, we naturally want to find a resolution. Because of this, conflict can be the greatest form of hooking a reader. Your story's beginning must have a conflict present in the very first chapter. The conflict doesn't necessarily need to be the main conflict of the story, but it should at the very least foreshadow the storm on the horizon for your main characters.

Hook #4: Genre/Setting

The setting that introduces your story can be a powerful hook if the author puts enough thought into the moment. Just as with characterization, you can find a way to grab the reader's attention by showing something that breaks expectations. If you're writing fantasy/sci-fi definitely consider showing off a cool element of your world.

Marissa Meyer's novel *Cinder* does this so well. The story opens with a seemingly normal girl working at a market. Immediately, the reader assumes this will be your average fairytale world until automatons and robotic engineering come into play. Meyer takes our pre-conceived expectations and squashes them like a bug on a windshield.

Hook #5: Narrative Voice

Would you believe that narration can be a hook? It totally can! If your reader enjoys the style of storytelling and feels as though the narrator—be it first or third person—is someone with whom they'd like to embark on an adventure, then that can be an extremely powerful hook. Great narration is concise, witty, and flows so the reader doesn't have to work hard to join the story.

I like to think of good narration as a transportation device.

Hooks are only part of what makes a successful beginning.

> **Travel Log Note**: As a writer, I *love* metaphors, but sometimes I piece them together in a very literal sense in my mind. Right now all I can think about is some teenager being pulled through the water by a good book hook. Do you ever do this? No? Okay. Moving on…

Once we have our reader on the metaphoric hook, we also need to make certain our beginning chapter provides the reader with enough information to reel them in.

By the end of the first chapter we should know the following:
- The genre
- What the protagonist wants
- Why they want it (motivation)
- A hint at the main conflict of the story

Plotting Pit Stop #2
The Springboard

Have you ever tried to steal someone's bounce on a trampoline? If you time it just right, you can allow someone else's momentum spring you into the air higher than you ever could have traveled on your own.

The springboard of the story has been referred to as the "catalyst" or "inciting incident" in other plotting methods. It is the moment in your story that propels your character into action. This is usually an external event that forces your protagonist to face a problem introduced at the beginning of the story. It is the moment your character must decide if they will roll over and live with the consequences of the springboard moment, or if they will take action and attempt to become the hero or heroine they were meant to be.

This plot point usually takes place once the author has established a good "before shot" of what the protagonist's normal life is like. The reader is invested in the character, has an idea of the major internal and external conflicts of the story, and then BOOM! the springboard moment launches the conflict like a 200-pound man launching a two-year-old on a trampoline, upping the stakes and forcing the main character into some kind of action.

In *Star Wars*, Luke Skywalker's springboard moment came when he saw the message with Princess Leia. In Gail Carson Levine's novel *Ella Enchanted*, it was the day Ella's father remarried. In the movie *Monsters Inc*, it comes after Sulley's arch rival Randall leaves a closet door open on the scream factory floor. It is the moment Prim's name is drawn as the District 12 tribute for the Hunger Games.

Consider some of the most recent books or movies you've read or watched. Can you identify the springboard moment near the beginning of the story that sets the rest of the story into motion?

As you plan for this springboard moment, keep in mind that the decision your hero makes after the springboard will mean so much more if there is sacrifice attached. In other words, the decision to set off on this adventure (whether literally like Frodo Baggins's choice to become the ring bearer in Lord of the Rings or figuratively like Hazel's decision to start attending group therapy in *The Fault in Our Stars*) will mean so much more if the choice isn't an easy, obvious one.

If the main character has a safer alternative to the one that is morally right, the ultimate decision will mean so much more. The hero shines not by the action of the springboard moment but by the humanity of debating which road is best in the aftermath. The decision should make them appear relatable *and* heroic.

> **Travel Log Note**: Giving your character tough choices is a great way to add tension to a story! We're going to talk about this more in Chapter 5.

Plotting Pit Stop #3
Reaching the Summit

Imagine driving my little Tercel up the Teton pass. The progress up the hill is slow, the gear low, but right when you crest the mountain summit, the speed changes. This turning point at the summit marks the moment of the story when the character shifts from playing defense to playing offense. This decision is usually marked by a big (false) victory or a big defeat in the story.

The victory feels real for a moment but opens the door for defeat in the end. When Cinderella goes to the ball and dances with the handsome prince, this feels like a huge moment of victory for her, but when the clock strikes midnight, the moment is proven an illusion and Cinderella's sad life is made worse. Now she not only has to work as a slave in her own home, but also has to do so while in love with a man whom she believes she'll never see again.

The summit is the moment in the story when the protagonist decides it's time to give up the one thing that has been holding them back. In Cinderella's case, she gives up a portion of her subservient nature and starts to defy her stepmother and stepsisters.

This pit stop may be the hardest to define because it can take on many forms and sits squarely in that murky middle of the book. The most important thing to remember is that reaching the summit is a big event that changes the way the character thinks. It is the metaphoric summit that causes a shift in the story, speeding the main character toward the climax while upping the stakes and increasing the pacing of the story.

Plotting Pit Stop #4
The Head-On Collision

For any victory to mean something, it must come by difficult means. The head-on collision is the moment in the story when the antagonist has his/her/its moment of glory. It is the moment when all of the efforts of the protagonist add up and are found lacking.

This is the moment in the story when it's best that the reader and the author are not sitting in the same room, otherwise the reader might get a little violent. ☺

Great authors are masters at weaving a story in such a way that when the head-on collision happens, they manage not just to mortally wound all hope of resolution for the characters, but do it in such a personal, insult-to-injury kind of way that the damage feels impossible to overcome.

> **Travel Log Note**: Writers really are the worst kind of sociopaths. *Literarily* speaking, of course.

How can we authors bring our characters to such a low place?

Simple. We know what they want more than anything else in this world *and* we know the most painful way to keep it from them. We've shown the reader this as well—taught them to love our hero/heroine to the point of being desperate to see them obtain their noble goal.

This head-on collision is a singular event that you've carefully prepped the reader for throughout the entire novel. It is the lowest of lows, the moment the reader is convinced marks the end of the protagonist's quest for happiness. It is a moment of painful, very personal (false) defeat.

Plotting Pit Stop #5
The Victory

Just when it appears all is lost, the victory comes when the main character digs down deep and finds a last thread of strength to win the day. By this point in the story, we should see a mighty change in the character. There should be a measure of sacrifice made, a change in heart, an inner strength discovered.

The victory will feel cheap if the solution comes too easy. Gone are the days when the fair princess has to wait for her handsome prince to save her. The princess better use that head of hers and become part of the solution, or she, as a character, falls flat. There is no sacrifice involved in being miraculously saved. Also, beware of using a character's hidden talents that haven't already been exposed throughout the story.

For example, if the princess suddenly knows how to throw knives like an expert, it feels too convenient. This section is where characters often move forward with courage *despite* of their limitations, rather than magically becoming something they are not.

The best victory moments come when the protagonist conquers an external conflict by overcoming an internal conflict. For example, let's pretend your story is about a group of friends that goes white water rafting. The main character's big internal conflict is that he is struggling to forgive another friend for a major wrong committed against them. The external conflict is the team is trying to be the first group to successfully run a deadly stretch of river.

Throughout the book we've seen how much our hero dislikes this person they used to call a friend. We see glimpses of their history, justifying the anger of our hero. Just as they are about to pull through the most dangerous part of the river, the boy our hero can't seem to forgive falls into the water. The victory now has two elements—an external and internal way for our hero to win the day. He saves his childhood friend and, in the processes, realizes that he can overcome his resentments and forgive.

Any way you can make the victory mean more to the reader is a huge bonus!

Plotting Pit Stop #6
The Final Destination

Endings are my favorite element of story structure. They are the payoff moment that both reader and—perhaps especially—writer have battled to reach over the course of the book. Good endings must accomplish a few important things.

First, they *must* resolve the main conflict of the story. Now, I know what you're thinking… what if the book is part of a series and is meant to be left as a cliff-hanger? That's totally okay. In *Nameless*, I end the book with my main characters in a sticky situation, but I do so after resolving the main conflict of the story. I can't say more without spoilers, but I can say that the reader finishes the book with a victory over the "big problem" that has kept the reader turning pages up to that point. If you deny your readers a victory or some kind of resolution that leaves your characters stronger and changed, then you're going to tick people off.

> **Travel Log Note**: I truly believe that when a reader picks up a book, an unspoken but profound contract between author and reader begins. The reader agrees to follow the main characters through fire and the writer agrees to provide the ending that makes everything worth it.

Second, the ending must show the new normal for both the world and the characters. The ending is basically a new beginning for your characters. It is your way of showing how life will continue after "The End." I always enjoy books that have an element of the story making a complete circle back to the beginning. I like the contrast it provides: the world before and the new and improved world now.

If you've ever seen the old classic Disney movie *Newsies* you see the opening image as a bunch of cute boys dancing and singing about selling "papes." Through the course of the story, the boys form a union and fight the financial giant, Pulitzer, and through much toil and loss come out champions. The victory moment is epic, with Jack riding out with Teddy Roosevelt, just like he bragged about doing in the beginning of the movie. The ending comes much like the beginning—with a bunch of boys dancing and singing and selling "papes." The world has changed because they will make more money than before, but life goes on. Great resolution and great ending!

Third, the ending must resolve all plot threads with secondary characters. The reader should never be left to wonder, "What ever happened to Aunt Sally's bakery?" Okay, perhaps that was a lame example, but you get my point. Any conflict not addressed in the ending that is meant to be left for a future book must still be briefly mentioned. The reader should have confidence in knowing the author didn't just forget, but that the resolution is coming.

Hit the Road: Plotting Framework
Writing Prompt

Identify the six pit stops of your novel:
1. The Starting Line
2. The Springboard
3. Reaching the Summit
4. Head-On Collision
5. The Victory
6. The Final Destination

5

The Fuel That Keeps Things Moving

I watch Dad flex his big hands on the steering wheel from my seat in the throne of the camper. We call it the throne because it's the one place in the camper that connects to the cab of the truck. The pathway from the kid's domain to the adults. I love this seat because even though it requires ducking my head and sandwiching my body to peek into the cab, I get to listen to the '80s music that rattles through the old speakers of the truck.

"What's wrong?" I ask because it's obvious from my father's tense body language and the absence of the smile lines around his eyes that something is, in fact, wrong.

Mom answers for him. "Grandpa likes to drive the speed limit."
And then I understand.

Trailing behind us, my grandparents are driving our second car so Mom doesn't have to follow. Grandma and Grandpa flew out to New Hampshire from their home in Utah to help with the cross-country caravan for this move.

I know Mom is grateful. She always complains about following Dad as he speeds to make good time on long trips. With no way of contacting him should she lose him on the road, she panics if even one car separates them on the freeway. (No cellphones, remember?)

"I can't take it anymore." Dad punches the gas.

"Lloyd!" my mom shrieks.

I can only imagine my grandpa, shouting the same exclamation at the same time. He's about to learn why Mom hates to drive the second car.

We drive like we're escaping a tidal wave for at least ten miles. Then Dad pulls off the road and brakes hard. I hear the telltale thump of bodies as Whitney and Josh crash against the front windows of the camper—a sure sign they hadn't braced in time.

"Rookies," I mutter.

"Everyone out!" Dad calls to his troops and we all file out—Mom included—to get our marching orders.

Dad grabs the football from under the seat and we immediately know what to do. Josh and I start running, laughing and shoving to catch the first pass. Whitney puts our Alaskan Malamute on his leash and shakes her head at our display. Three years my junior and Whitney is more mature than I will ever be. In all of our shoving, neither Josh nor I catch the football, but it doesn't matter, because we're out of the camper, stretching our legs, breathing air that hasn't been filtered through the old truck/camper vents.

Eventually Grandpa and Grandma drive by. Grandma stares in shock at the band of us playing football on the shoulder of the freeway.

"Jump in!" Dad calls, and we file in, dog and all.

It's not long before we pass my grandparents again.

As we do, we pretend to wave at the strangers in the other direction, pretending we don't see my grandparents, just because we think we're funny, and the game continues for the rest of the day. Speed. Stop. Football. Repeat. It's the fasted and slowest drive we've ever had and I love every minute.

Have you ever read a book that dragged? The book sounded interesting when you read the description, but after the first chapter you just couldn't get into the story?

I've spent a lot of time trying to understand why some stories drag and others have me turning pages into the wee hours of the morning.

There are a lot of factors that create a page-turner, but I think Lee Child, the famous suspense author of the Jack Reacher series, said it best.

On December 8, 2012, Child was featured as a guest blogger for the New York Times *Opinionator*. He wrote that building suspense doesn't have a magical checklist or recipe for success. You can't just add a cup of good characterization, a dash of cliff-hangers, a red herring, and then set the timer to bake for thirty minutes.

Building tension and suspense is actually much less complicated.

Child says the secret of building tension in a story can be summed up in one question: How do you make your family hungry?

The answer is simple. You make them wait four hours for dinner.

Tension is built by the author posing a question and then delaying the answer. Most questions authors pose are not stated with a question mark. Instead, the question is inferred by including details that build curiosity so the reader is constantly asking themselves, "Why did they do that? What is going to happen? Do I trust them?" etc.

There are many ways to inspire curiosity in a reader. We lay the foundation for suspense and tension in the first chapter of the story—that first pit stop meant to hook your reader.

> **Travel Log Note**: I talk about hooks and the first pit stop in Chapter 4. I'd repeat myself here, but that might slow the pacing of this chapter. ☺

The Art of Unpredictability

Authors can create tension by taking away the reader's ability to predict the outcome of a scene, the decision-making of a character, or the solution to the main conflict of the story. There is a balance between being unpredictable to a fault and setting the reader up for a satisfying surprise.

Here are some DO'S and DON'Ts of unpredictability:

1. DON'T introduce a "fix-it" character or tool late in the story.
For the solution of the conflict to mean anything to the reader, it must come at the hands of established characters. Introducing a mentor charac-

ter at the eleventh hour or perhaps even a magic pill that will solve everything bleeds all of the tension out of the story and cheapens your characters' victory.

This does not mean you can't have a mentor character or a magical "fix-it" tool to assist your character(s) on their quest for a happy ending. It just means that help shouldn't just appear out of thin air without proper foreshadowing.

A good example of this comes from *Harry Potter and the Prisoner of Azkaban.* Hermione doesn't just happen to have a Time-Turner (a magical object that allows her to go back in time). Instead, Rowling establishes over the course of the book that Hermione is mysteriously taking more classes than seems possible. Harry and Ron wonder how she manages to take two different classes taught at the same time, but the matter is left unexplained until the need for the Time-Turner comes in line with the major crisis of the plot.

As messy as time-travel can be, the Time-Turner would have appeared *way* too convenient had Hermione not been using it throughout the course of the story. The foreshadowing was solid *and* the Time-Turner itself didn't solve everything, but instead made the climax of the story possible. Harry still had to find the power to conjure a *patronus* powerful enough to scare away a hoard of Dementors.

> **Travel Log Note**: If you've never read the third Harry Potter, I've likely just used about ten words that confuse you. That might be frustrating, and I apologize for that. *But go read the stinking book!* It's amazing.

2. DO use red herrings!

A red herring is a literary device that intentionally leads readers to a false conclusion, distracting them from truth. I like to think of them as the flashy gesture a magician makes with one hand while his other hand is tucking a card up his sleeve.

Red herrings can be characters, such as a decoy for a villain or the sorry loser in a love triangle. They can also be the perceived "only solution" to a problem. Whether the red herring is the nice guy that's just a little too nice or the villain whose actions don't quite measure up, this device can add a sense of unpredictability and tension to the story because it causes the reader to doubt their preconceived notions. Doubt = Unpredictability

> **Travel Log Note**: People debate the origin of the "red herring" idiom. While there isn't an actual red herring swimming around in the ocean, there are fish called herrings that, when heavily salted and smoked, turn red. Red herrings may have been used to help train hunting dogs as a decoy scent from the goal of a fox or deer. The salted and smoked herring was dragged perpendicular to the scent the dogs were suppose to follow as a test to see if they could stick with the original scent without becoming distracted. Just a little salted food for thought.

3. DON'T give up your secrets too quickly.

An author's job is to create in the reader a desire to chase after resolution. For this to work, the author must have a few big secrets in his or her back pocket. Going into the story, the author should know a great deal about the character—secrets the character would like to hold close to their chest. These secrets should be hinted at throughout the course of the story as clever clues for the reader to follow.

Too often new writers feel the need to give the reader way too much information and backstory at the beginning of the book. Novice authors are afraid to hint at history, worried the reader will get too confused. Readers are smart! They want to chase after the history and secrets of characters. It's one of the best parts of the reading experience. Remember the common saying, "Curiosity may have killed the cat, but it also turned the page."

4. DO incorporate plot twists into your story!

A great plot twist has the reader nodding their head saying "Wow!" and not scratching it saying "What in the world...?" Also known as "reversals," plot twists are the epitome of unpredictability. If executed effectively, the reader should be able to go back and spot clues that fore-shadowed the twist but were also subtle enough to be overlooked during the first read.

A plot twist might be a moment when a protagonist's close friend be-trays him—or, on the flip side, the moment a villain saves the protagonist's life and joins her side. These can be a lot of fun for the au-thor. Be creative and don't forget to use your "What if?" questions to challenge your existing story for potential plot twists.

Changing Speeds

Building up tension in a story is not unlike blowing air into a balloon. With every scene the pressure on the main character(s) to succeed should increase. For example, if you open the book with a planet exploding, the whole galaxy should be in danger by the end.

Does that mean that the characters should never have any down time to regroup?

Not at all.

In fact, pushing the pedal to the metal the entire "drive" can become exhausting and cheapen the true big moments for the reader. Characters need time to debate or reflect on their situation so when the action does come, it means more. This time of reflection often adds depth to character that it difficult to achieve during action scenes.

Just like my cross-country travel with grandparents, your reader will appreciate a variety of bursts and pauses along the way, all while continu-ing to inflate that balloon.

Multiple Plotlines

Introducing multiple plotlines to a story is a huge way of guaranteeing that your tension is building while letting characters "take turns" in the spot-light. Great writers add dimension to secondary characters so they can have their time to shine when the main plot of the story is building.

The whole source of any kind of plot is captured in a character's de-sire. We discussed this in detail in Chapter 2, but I'll say it again, because it bears repeating: If you can create a desire in your character, you can easily create a plot.

Examine your secondary characters. Is there something they might be missing from life—something personal that is independent from the main conflict of the story? If so, BOOM! Build on that, create events that showcase the character's "lack," make them fail a few times, create a moment when all is lost and they're ready to quit, and then—preferably during the climax of the story—have them achieve their heart's desire in an awesome way. BAM! You have a subplot.

> **Travel Log Note**: Sorry to keep shouting at you with explosion references. I'm still thinking about planets superheating and vaporizing. ☺

Once you have a few good subplots in mind, look at your plot. I like to map it out on a graph, marking the major events of the story where I know my tension levels are high. I'll stick with the exploding planet concept to illustrate my point.

In this story let's pretend that our protagonist is a teenage girl named Nova Star. Her story represents our main plot line. Other prominent subplots follow the story of our villain, Callister Lab, as well as Nova's love interest, Ronnie "Danger" Fly.

Notice on the graph that I've noted the level of tension for each subplot during each chapter.

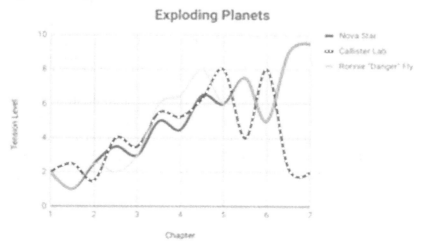

Exploding Planets

I call this process of graphing *tension testing*. (And you thought you'd never use those graphs you learned in science class.)

Mapping out the tension levels of your story is extremely helpful in finding weak areas that would benefit from subplots. It is important to realize that tension can come from a variety of scenes and situations. It might be a first kiss, if you're writing a romance novel. It might be finding a dead body that cracks open a murder investigation in a mystery novel. Or it might be a big action scene your reader has been anticipating throughout the book.

I rate the scenes in my tension test high if they are "payoff" moments, as opposed to "building" moments.

Examples:

Training for battle = building moment
Fighting the battle = payoff moment

Having a first date = building moment
Experiencing first kiss = payoff moment

Studying for the ACT = building moment
Receiveing a college acceptance letter = payoff moment

Building moments are not less important than payoff moments. Often they are vital to enhance the progress of the plot. More importantly, they are the moments that make the payoff *mean* something.

After you've taken the time to create your subplots, couple building moments in your main plotline with payoff moments from your subplots. Be creative. You will likely surprise yourself by how complex your plot is growing.

Once you've puzzled the events together, add them to your tension test, giving each subplot it's own new line, as shown in the graph.

Imagine having three different kettles of water on a stove and heating them at different temperatures. They are all getting hotter with every passing minute. They won't all produce steam at the same time, but by the end, all of the kettles will be whistling

Creating Powerful Payoff Moments

Now that you know where the high-suspense payoff moments land in your story, you'll want to be sure to do them justice. If you've left enough breadcrumbs and piqued your reader's curiosity enough, they should be dying to devour those payoff moments. Now you need to flex those author-ly muscles of yours and deliver.

Let's say you're writing a story about a man with little money who's in love with a wealthy debutante promised to another man whom she does not love. We spend a great part of the story building up the romantic connection of our poor hero and his unattainable girl. They fall in love and the couple decides to elope, agreeing to meet at the train station at dawn.

The trouble is, the girl's fiancé discovers their plans and snatches the gun from the case on his wall and sets off to intercept them thinking, *If he can't have her, no one can.*

The lovers spot each other through a cloud of steam. They have no idea the murderous fiancé is hiding behind a pillar with gun raised…

This is the point when the author needs to slow everything down. We've spent a great deal of time building up tension for this event, but now, in the moment of payoff, we take our time, slowing time to describe every detail of what happens next. The click of the gun as the hammer is pulled back, the relieved smile of the lovers when they spot each other, internal dialogue from the narrator expressing how he or she can't wait to spend the rest of their lives together, etc. The details of the kiss that finally give the villain the rage that propels him to pull the trigger, the weight of the girl's body as she falls in our hero's arms, the spread of blood mixing with the condensation on the platform.

I think you get my point.

Once the moment has passed, you should speed everything back up to normal time, just like a roller-coaster slowing at the summit of a big climb and then speeding into a drop.

This method of writing payoff moments will satisfy the reader and give them the shock they've been anticipating throughout the book.

Hit the Road: Tension Test
Writing Prompt

Part One: Create a tension test graph by plotting the building moments and payoff moments for your protagonist(s). Then do the same thing for your secondary characters. If possible, see if you can have the tension peak for all plotlines in the climax of your story.

Part Two: Brainstorm ideas for plot twists and red herrings using "What if" questions. Don't limit your imagination. You may find some great ways to add tension to your plot and discover some secrets for your characters that will have readers turning pages.

6

Stop Arguing With Your Brother: Writing Punchy Dialogue

"I will pull this thing over!" Dad's threat barely reaches us. It's the third time we've been warned, but my brother and I are at war, and neither of us knows the meaning of surrender.

My family traded in the Colt Vista for an old Chevy Truck with a camper that fits like a Tetris piece in the back. Dining room, bathroom, and kitchen make up the main floor of our mobile palace. We lay up above the cab of the truck where a full-sized bed with duct-taped windows provides views of the Rocky Mountains.

I tug hard on the blanket Josh stole from me five minutes ago. "I said, give it back!" My words are a growl. It's unconfirmed but I'm pretty sure my Patronus is a grizzly. Especially in January in an old camper that has gaps that allow currents of arctic air to pass through.

> **Travel Log Note**: Did you know a male grizzly is called a boar and a female is called a sow? My brother once called me a sow, but I called him a bore.

"You can have it." A crooked grin stretches across my brother's face. "If you can take it." He holds the blanket locked in his fists. The "I Have Something You Want" game is one of his favorites. Rivaled only by the "Fart in Your Face and Run" game.

Even though he is older, I've played this game as long as he has, and he knows I'm up for the challenge. I go for a diversion tactic and knuckle-punch him in the leg a split-second before I tug. He's ready for this and drives his heel into my side.

I press my feet into his chest and grip the blanket with two hands as I try to straighten my legs and rip it from his grubby paws. By this time, our little sister has fled to the lower level of the camper—smart girl.

Inch by inch, I gain a little more blanket. I am winning and I sense my victory like a shark in bloody water.

As I brace for one final pull, Josh is ready for me. He releases his hold just as I give a Braveheart-worthy battle cry and tug with all I have. I careen into the wall and smack my head.

The camper screeches to a halt and Josh and I roll and collide into the front windows.

Shoot.

Dad's door opens and slams shut. I know it's Dad's because Mom doesn't have that kind of power. Josh and I both release the blanket at once.

I nudge my brother and whisper, "Now you've done it."

"If you weren't so loud," he hisses.

"You stole my blanket."

"We were having fun."

I shake my head, amazed that my brother and I share the same genetics.

We both startle when the door to the camper opens.

Dad stands just outside a doorway so narrow we can't see the full expanse of his broad shoulders. "Out."

Josh and I share a glance. This is uncharted territory for us. Dad is all about making good time. If we're stopping, we're in serious trouble.

"Now!"

We scramble down from the loft in a tangle of blankets and adolescent limbs.

"Shoes on," he commands. Snow flurries race behind him on a stiff breeze. There's a crazed look in his eyes that I've never seen before.

I double-knot my Converse All-Stars with the speed of a steer wrestler tying off a calf and jump outside, my brother right behind me. The cold mountain air slices through my hoodie and I'm instantly shivering.

Dad looks down on us in all his 6'5" glory. A car speeds past, honking because the road is narrow and the shoulder almost non-existent.

"It's a long drive." His voice is nearly swallowed up by the sound of yet another rushing car. "You two need to get your energy out."

"He stole my blanket."

"She overreacts."

Dad sighs and walks back to the driver's seat. He climbs inside, and I assume that's our cue to follow his example. Relief floods me. For a second there I thought we were in real trouble.

I step to the door of the camper, but the truck pulls away. My father must have lost his mind.

"We're not in yet!" I call up to him.

Dad sticks his head out the window and says, "I suggest you start running."

He speeds away, leaving my brother and I to stare with mouths gaping after him.

Remember how I mentioned lax seatbelt laws back in the '80s? Well, parenting practices were a little different back then too. Mom later told me she was worried about this creative punishment, but Dad thought he was a genius. What better way to have two quarreling kids blow off some steam than to have them run for what seemed like miles up a dangerous mountain road?

Though I don't remember the actual dialogue that transpired between my brother and I as we ran along that narrow, winding road, I do remember fighting over who had to run on the inside, nearest the rushing cars. Our dialogue began with shivered accusations and the occasional shove in the shoulder and ended with us laughing at the ridiculousness of our predicament.

Dad hadn't been bluffing or just trying to scare us by pulling out of sight around the first bend. Josh and I ended up running for a long time before we saw that ugly truck and camper again.

Principles of Authentic Dialogue

Dialogue is a vital weapon in the hands of a skilled writer. It naturally increases pacing, is humor's vehicle of choice, and provides a window into the mind of characters.

Logic would suggest that writing dialogue should be as easy as shifting a car into gear and pressing down on the gas pedal. We might not know what it's like to live on a space colony or battle a dragon, but talking to people and being part of a conversation is a huge part of our daily lives. So writing dialogue should be a no-brainer.

Right?

Wrong!

Why? Because we speak differently than we should write.

Test this theory by paying attention to your next phone conversation.

Dear Teen Reader: A phone conversation differs greatly from a text conversation. Even though your parents don't want me to tell you this, in some ways, texting more closely resembles proper written dialogue than speaking. Stay tuned and I'll explain.

Let's pretend you are calling up your crush to invite him to a movie. If I wrote this scene the way we conventionally speak to one another, it might sound like this.

Ring, ring.

"Hello?"

"Hi, Steven. It's Jen. How are you?"

"I'm good. How are you?"

"I'm good. Hey, a few of us are going to see that scary movie about the kids abducted while running on the side of the road. It's supposed to be awesome. Do you want to come?"

"What time is the movie?"

"7:00. We'd pick you up around 6:30."

"Let me check with my mom."

Silence for a few moments and then Steven comes back on the line and says, "Yes. I can go."

"Great. See you then."

Wasn't it boring to read through those greetings? Didn't both Steven and Jen sound like they had zero personality? They're probably going to have a very boring time at the movie.

This brings us to our first rule of dialogue.

Rule #1: Dialogue is best boiled.

If you boiled a can of Coke, eventually all of the water would evaporate, leaving you with thick, syrupy goo. Good dialogue has all of the boring parts boiled away. This means communicating as much as you can in as few words as possible.

Here's another version of the scene from above with the "fluff" of the dialogue boiled away. I've added some action for added appeal.

Ring, ring.

"Hello?" asks Steven.

"It's Jen."

Steven smiles into the phone. "Which Jen? There's like a hundred of you."

"Very funny. I was going *to invite you to the scary movie about the kids abducted on the side of the road. It's supposed to be awesome, but since you don't know me…"*

"Oh, that Jen!" He can't fight the laugh any longer. "What time?"

"Pick you up around 6:30?"

Steven doesn't move the phone from his mouth as he shouts to his mom in the other room. Jen hates when he does that. His pathetic grin makes the question harder for his lips to form, but this is Jen. How can he not smile?

Mom says yes and Steven tries not to sound too excited when he tells her, "I'm in."

Travel Log Note: I actually don't recommend boiling Coke at home. Your parent will likely not appreciate the experiment. Take my word for it...

Rule #2: Dialogue shouldn't be used to "tell" action.

If your dialogue rehashes events that have already taken place or is commentating on events that are happening in real time (instead of showing the action), then your reader will lose interest. I refer to this type of poor storytelling as *commentary dialogue.*

Here's an example of commentary dialogue:

Josh shoves me away. "You are running so close to me that your elbow is brushing mine. I don't want to touch you. Back off!"

"Don't you see these cars racing past? I don't want to be hit," I shout.

"Well, maybe you should have thought about that before screaming for your blanket like a little baby in the car."

Did you notice how Josh's dialogue told the reader what was happening instead of the narrator *showing* the action play out? This lazy dialogue limits the imagination of the reader, sucking away all description and emotion until only a sad, skeletal window into the action of the scene remains.

Let's fix that last scene so that our readers can have a chance to discover the details without being told.

Josh shoves me closer to the yellow line separating me from potential traffic. "Stop elbowing me," he says.

I shove him back just as a large truck and trailer round the bend. The rumbling vehicle breezes past us, whipping my ponytail and churning the arctic air into a violent whirl. "Are you trying to kill me?" I'm shivering so hard the words are stiff and nearly unintelligible.

"Don't give me any ideas," he mumbles even as he runs a fraction closer to the cliff to make room for me.

Take time to examine your dialogue scenes to check for commentary dialogue. With a little tweaking, weakness in dialogue can quickly become strength.

Rule #3: Communication is messy and messy is interesting.

Guess what? When it comes to dialogue, you don't have to write complete sentences. Interesting conversations are often filled with interruptions, pauses, and misdirection. Let your characters answer questions with questions. Let them talk over one another or pause when things get awkward.

Interruptions or pauses in dialogue can be as important as the words spoken. They can convey fear, lies, hope, reluctance, and a full range of other emotions.

- "I miss you, Anne," Weston said.
- "I… miss you, Anne," Weston said.
- "I miss you... Anne!" Weston said.

What was Weston thinking in those pauses? Uncertainty? Perhaps desperation?

Master writers use dialogue to help characters say more than the words that lie between the quotation marks. Pauses, misdirection, one-word responses, and unanswered questions help us feel as though a character isn't a robot, programmed to ask questions in complete sentences. So feel free to break rules of conventional speech. Hey, we don't call it creative writing for nothing.

Rule #4: Pay attention to subtext.

Subtext—literally what's happening underneath ("sub") the actual words the character is speaking—is all about emotion and motivation. It explains why the character is saying something. Subtext engages the reader in a powerful process of discovery: what are the characters' motives, what they are thinking, what is happening or has happened in this world that makes a character act this way.

For example, note the difference between Ron Weasley saying, "I dislike you, Malfoy!" and saying, "Eat slugs!"

We can tell how Ron feels about Malfoy by his word choice. We recognize these characters have a history of bad feelings for each other. And going back to Rule #1, "Eat slugs!" is punchy, effective, and uses half the words of the alternative.

The purpose of subtext is to make the dialogue mean more than what is actually said. Jealousy, confusion, anger, pride, fear, love—all should and can be *shown* (through dialogue and action) instead of told.

> **Travel Log Note**: We will discuss the vital skill of *showing* instead of *telling* in Chapter 7.

Rule #5: Dialogue should sound like the character speaking.
Speech patterns reveal a great deal about characters and can help you avoid long paragraphs of description. Remember *show, don't tell*? Age, gender, region, ethnicity or nationality, level of education—all can be conveyed by the way a character speaks.

- "How are you doing today?"
- "Well, how the heck are ya?"
- "S'up?"
- "I trust you are feeling well?"

Big difference, right? We're essentially asking the same question, but through the voice of four very different characters.

Before you start writing a piece of dialogue, be sure to ask yourself, "How would my character react in this moment? What words would he or she use to express emotions?"

Here's a little game I like to call "Which Harry Potter Character Said…" See if you can guess who is speaking in each of the dialogue lines below:

1. "Gotta bone ter pick with yeh. I've heard you've bin givin' out signed photos. How come I haven't got one?"
2. "Oh Harry, don't you see? If she could have done one thing to make absolutely sure that every single person in this school will read your interview, it was banning it!"
3. "My father told me all the Weasleys have red hair, freckles, and more children than they can afford."

4. "Yes, it is easy to see that nearly six years of magical education have not been wasted on you, Potter. 'Ghosts are transparent'."

5. "I enjoyed the meetings, too. It was like having friends."

J. K. Rowling does a fantastic job of using dialogue to add depth and dimension to her characters. No two characters sound the same (with the obvious and intentional exception of Fred and George).

*Answers for the Potter Dialogue Quiz can be found at the end of this chapter.

Rule #6: Braid dialogue with action and description.

Good dialogue is supported by action and description. For example, notice how when we attach different actions to the same dialogue it creates subtext and changes the meaning of the words:

- "I love you, Sam." Sara studied the ground as she drew a circle in the sand with her shoe.
- "I love you, Sam." Sara pounded his chest with her clinched fists and dared him to look away.
- "I love you, Sam." Sara covered her face to hide her tears.
- "I love you, Sam." Sara pinched his cheek as though he were five and walked away.

See? "I love you" can be shyly hopeful, passionate and demanding, teasing, or even tortured. All it takes is adding the right action to your dialogue.

Description, like action, can also set the mood for the dialogue and scene. A few carefully chosen words can guide your reader to the right state of mind. If our characters are in a forest setting and the conversation is meant to be threatening, we might describe the crunch of dead leaves beneath our character's shifting feet or the rattling of branches in the wind to break up the dialogue. In that same forest setting, if the dialogue exchange is meant to be a playful or happy, perhaps our character will notice the sunlight filtering through the forest canopy or the scent of pine in the air.

Thoughtful details act as a framework for dialogue and support the message you send your reader. Often description provides enough support to the scene that actual dialogue is less important. This is especially important with action scenes. Too much dialogue can turn into cliché monologuing.

In the following scene, notice how the dialogue takes a backseat to description.

Lights from the Tilt-o-Whirl blur before my eyes as I stumble forward. A young child yells, "I want a candy apple!" while tugging on the hand of his mother.

I blink hard, trying to force the ground to stay still as I struggle to keep my balance. The clickity-clack *of the wooden rollercoaster just ahead precedes the sudden screams of thrill-seekers.*

I blink hard as faces dance in the corners of my vision, distorted and inhuman.

"I'm sorry it had to be this way," D'Angelo says next to me.

I look down at the drink in my unsteady hand. The drink D'Angelo bought for me right before I told him about the money. My hand shakes so hard I drop the plastic cup. Soda explodes upon impact, causing shrieks from passersby that grate along my spine.

"Why?" My mouth is cotton. I turn to find that D'Angelo is no longer next to me.

Noise bounces sprays of reds and golds and blues across my vision.

My knees buckle and I strike the ground like a domino: knees, elbows, head.

Rule #7: Dialogue exchanges can (and often should) have a winner and a loser.

Dialogue is often a power struggle that demands a winner and a loser. You can achieve this by rethinking the way you approach creating a scene. Instead of polite back-and-forth discussions, try to incorporate confrontations, arguments, teasing, or misunderstandings.

In the introductory scene for this chapter, the clear winner of the dialogue exchange was my father when he said, "I suggest you start running." My brother and I carried the majority of the scene, but my father had the upper hand because his line packed the biggest punch. It is not necessary for your characters to be arguing to have a winner or a loser. Often, though not always, the winner is the character who has the last word or a big "mic drop" line. The winner might also be the person who makes the aggressor stop and think. If the proper subtext is provided, the winner can even be the person who says nothing at all.

In my YA fantasy novel *Nameless*, my heroine infiltrates the fearsome Ram Clan as a spy and a slow-burn love story ensues between her and an enemy warrior. Notice in the following dialogue exchange that there is a clear winner.

Gryphon looked away, grateful for the cover of night. "Despite what you think, I am not a monster."

"No." Zo picked up her kit from the ground and wiped blood from the corner of her mouth. "You are a Ram."

Keeping the "winner vs. loser" struggle in mind will help you add tension to your dialogue. And tension keeps readers turning the page.

Dialogue Tags and Mechanics

It is vital that your reader understands who is talking in your story. The most obvious way to do this is to provide dialogue tags.

Dialogue Tags

"What is a dialogue tag?" **asked James**.

"I'll tell you," **Susan said**.

A dialogue tag is a clause (think incomplete sentence) of two words or more that attributes the dialogue to the speaker.

Allow me to introduce you to the invisible "he said" and "she said" and their cousin "asked." We glue these tags to the front, back or even sometimes middle of a line of dialogue to make it clear who is speaking. I call them invisible because they are the most subtle way of tagging a character and should be used the majority of the time. Why? Because they know how to get out of the way.

I'll explain.

There are hundreds of dialogue tags that have an action attached—he cried, she whimpered, he begged, she shouted, he whispered, etc. The list goes on and on. All of these tags serve the purpose of identifying the speaker, but writers should be careful not to use these types of tags too often. Instead of relying on these action tags, writers should try to use action to show crying instead of simply stating "she cried," or show whimpering instead of "she whimpered."

Compare the two dialogue passages:

- "Please, sir. My husband is innocent," **the woman begged**.
- "Please, sir," **the woman said**, dropping to her knees and pressing her forehead to the earth. "My husband is innocent."

The second passage is so much better because we can visualize the woman begging through her actions.

If you want to get really crazy, you can actually show who is speaking by not using a tag at all.

- "Please, sir." The woman dropped to her knees and pressed her forehead to the earth. "My husband is innocent."

The action sentence sandwiched between the dialogue sentences suggests that "the woman" is speaking, so no tag is necessary. Cool, right?

The words you choose and the actions you attach can help you get rid of flowery dialogue tags and make your writing stronger.

Beware the –ly Adverb

Dialogue tags attached to -ly adverbs (i.e., *she said **sadly*** or *he asked **miserably***) are often looked upon as a missed opportunity. Yes, they make it very easy to add subtext and emotion to the dialogue, but they pack a weaker punch than solid description and action.

Compare the following examples.

"Adam, you passed the test!" Sam said excitedly.

"Adam, you passed the test!" Sam threw his binder in the air. Loose homework pages flitted to the ground around them like over-sized confetti.

The first example uses the –ly adverb "excitedly" while the second example relies on action and description to show excitement. Remember, good writers want their reader to feel as though they are right in the action. They try to *show* readers a scene instead of *telling* them a story.

Punctuation and Dialogue

Yes, I said it. The nasty "P" word that makes so many writers cringe. Luckily, the rules for punctuation in dialogue are pretty straightforward.

Start a new paragraph when someone new is speaking.

Easy enough, right? Here is an example pulled from the introductory story in this chapter:

I nudge my brother and whisper, "Now you've done it."
"If you weren't so loud," he hisses.
"You stole my blanket."
"We were having fun."
I shake my head, amazed that my brother and I share the same genes.

Notice there is a clear paragraph break every time the speaker changes. Similar to dialogue tags, this helps the reader follow who is speaking. Because this is a tense moment in the story, and there are only two people involved in the conversation, the rapid-fire exchange at the end actually works well without tags.

Here's another example:

I tug hard on the blanket Josh stole from me a few minutes ago. "I said, give it back!" My words are a growl. It's unconfirmed but I'm pretty sure my Patronus is a Grizzly. Especially in January in an old camper that has gaps that allow currents of arctic air to pass through.

"You can have it." A crooked grin stretches across my brother's face. "If you can take it." He holds the blanket locked in his fists.

Notice the dialogue can share a paragraph with other sentences that provide description, action, and support what is being spoken. A new paragraph begins with the new speaker.

"Quotation marks outside punctuation, please."

We all know that dialogue should begin and end with quotation marks, but let's discuss the rules for other punctuation. Study the dialogue samples below and notice the subtle differences.

Use a comma to separate dialogue from dialogue tags. We do this because the tag is a subordinate clause and is tied to the dialogue. I used to panic when I read words like "subordinate clause" in school. In a nutshell, it just means that the tag depends on the dialogue to make it a complete sentence. In the following example, watch for the placement of the comma and quotation marks.

> *"This is how you punctuate using dialogue tags," the teacher said.*

Notice the comma comes **before** the quotation mark.

We use a period to punctuate dialogue that is followed by a complete sentence. Notice in this example that the dialogue is its own sentence and the action is its own sentence.

> *"This is how you punctuate without a dialogue tag." The teacher pointed to the example on the board.*

Again, the period comes **before** the quotation mark.

If your character is asking a question, a question mark should be used in place of a comma even when using a dialogue tag. As before, be sure to place the question mark **before** the quotation mark. The same rules apply for exclamation points.

> *"How do you punctuate a question using a dialogue tag?" he asked.*

A girl in the front row raised her hand. "Is it different than asking a question without a tag?"

Writers often like to break up dialogue by tagging or adding action mid-sentence. Here are a few examples:

"To punctuate a tag mid-sentence," he said, "you must separate dialogue from non-dialogue using quotation marks."
Notice the dialogue tag is not inside quotation marks.

*"Also," she said, pointing at the board, "**there** is no need to capital-ize the second half of a dialogue sentence that is broken up by a tag."*

In this case the word "there" is not capitalized because it is a continu-ation of the dialogue sentence.

See? That wasn't so bad, was it? If you ever find yourself struggling with punctuating dialogue, you can always open one of your favorite books to find a sentence similar to the one you're struggling to punctuate.

> **Travel Log Note**: Did you know that in Great Britain they use the single quote (') instead of the double (")? They also place their punctuation *after* the quotation mark, instead of before. 'How weird is that'?

Writing dialogue can and should be a lot of fun! It is your opportunity to let your readers get a greater glimpse into the minds of your characters. It also ups the tension and adds a nice break in description and action scenes. Remember to boil that dialogue down to only the necessary words. Keep things punchy and make certain someone walks away victorious from every conversation.

But maybe not too punchy. You don't want to find yourself running along the side of a mountain road.

Hit the Road: Dialogue Writing Prompt

Using the dialogue below, add action and description to strengthen the scene.

Sample Scene:

"Please don't kick me again," Tom said.

"Why not, fart-face? You going to stop me?" said Butch.

Sample Solution:

"Please don't kick me again." Tom huddled in the corner, hiding his broken nose with shaking hands.

A slow grin spread across Butch's face. "Why not, fart-face?" He leaned down. The full force of his sour breath hit Tom as hard as any fist. "You going to stop me?"

Dialogue #1

"Have you lost your mind?" Jane asked.

"It's worth the risk," said George.

Dialogue #2

"I wish you'd let me love you," said Bill.

"I wish you knew how," said Jenny.

Dialogue #3

"You can't take my stuff," Sam said.

"Trust me. This is the least of your problems, kid," said the officer.

Harry Potter Dialogue Answers:

1.Hagrid 2. Hermione Granger 3. Draco Malfoy 4. Professor Snape 5. Luna Lovegood

7

Taking the Scenic Route

"Wake up." I nudge Angela after filling the car with gas. "Your turn to drive. I'm going to fall asleep."

Three days ago, Angela and I drove to Las Vegas with her mother following in a separate car. Angela had recently moved from Vegas and was excited to introduce me to some of her old friends. We filled those days with a lot of laughter, night hiking, and tasting every flavor of Coca-Cola on the strip. On the last night, we didn't go to bed until 8:00 a.m.

I drove the first leg of the journey on only two hours of sleep.

Now, even under the shelter of the gas station's metal canopy, the rain flies sideways, pelting our exposed skin with unrelenting force as we run around the car to switch places.

Doors slam shut and I immediately buckle and recline my seat. With eyes heavy, head pounding from sleep deprivation, twilight descending, the rhythmic swishing of windshield wipers, and the white noise of the rain, I fall asleep almost instantly to the lullaby of "Cowboy, Take Me Away" by the Dixie Chicks.

I wake to the sound of Angela's scream.

I sit up to find the road is not stretching out in front of us as it should. The window above my passenger-side door has somehow become the new windshield. We are perpendicular to the road, hydroplaning at eighty miles per hour.

The tires blow out as they regain traction. The car catches on the asphalt, and we take flight.

The first flight is peaceful. We seem to float through the air. Centripetal force pushes my body back against the reclined seat. I hope Angela is buckled as my own belt cuts into my hips.

We land hard on my side of the car. Glass shatters all around us. Metal whines as it crunches into a new form, and we're suddenly airborne again.

Time slows.

I have the clear thought: I might die tonight.

Who will run the mail at the Thanksgiving Point offices if I don't report for work tomorrow?

If I die, I'll miss my next basketball game.

We land again, harder than the first time and again on my side of the car. The world is black but I am calm. I am firmly in the hands of the one who created me. We roll again, this time in a more violent, washing-machine-like tumble until we connect with something solid.

Everything stops but the pounding of my heart.

I take a moment to realize I am still alive before I remember my friend.

"Angela!" I mean to shout but my voice comes out as a squeaky cry.

The car is completely dark as I hang upside-down by my seat belt. The roof is now the floor and it seems too close. Not enough room to breathe. Why can't I breathe?

I fumble to release my seat belt. My body drops, but not far. The ceiling has collapsed. My passenger side window is completely pinched shut. How am I alive? If my chair hadn't been reclined...

I cut off the thought. I will get out of the car. I will breathe.

"Angela!" I call again, this time with more force.

"Jen!" she answers. "Can you get out?"

I start an army crawl toward the back seat of the car on the driver's side. My arms and hands collect the glass that once belonged in the windows. When I finally free myself from the wreckage and feel the grass between my fingers I want to cry.

I climb to my feet.

Angela is there, her face already swelling. She has cuts along her arm and on the side of her face. I look down at my own cuts and gashes, amazed that I don't feel an ounce of pain even though some of the cuts look deep.

"I'm so glad you're not dead," Angela cries. We're too dazed to even attempt an embrace.

"Me too." I snort a laugh and she joins in. We're probably in shock. Or the sweetly strong and deadly stale smell of gasoline has addled our brains.

We're about a hundred yards from the road and I can see now that it was a cedar tree that finally stopped our car from rolling down the hill. The tree is practically cut in half.

"Your mom's going to freak," I add. She probably saw us go off the road since she was right behind us.

Angela picks up half of a broken disk off the ground. "My CDs!" she sobs and laughs at the same time. "Help me."

By the glow of the car's only remaining headlight, we shuffle along the rough ground, picking up the dozens of CDs that have scattered in our near-death tumble.

"My Spice Girls! It's dead." Angela holds up the broken remains of the disk.

I snort another laugh. So does she.

I barely register the sirens in the distance.

Definitely in shock, but it feels wrong not to celebrate survival.

Flashlight beams charge toward us.

My head starts to hurt and I sink to the ground, still reaching for CDs, my efforts slacking.

Somewhere nearby, Angela's mom shrieks in hysterics. I reach for another CD and notice a two-inch piece of glass poking out of the back of my hand.

Men in rescue gear advance toward the car carrying a large metal tool that resembles raptor claws. "I can't see anyone!" one shouts.

It takes a moment for me to realize they're looking for Angela and me.

"Over here!" I call.

Angela is still picking up CDs.

The men look at us, astonished. And I can understand why. The car is beyond totaled. No one should have survived.

I let the CDs slide from my lap as they rush over. Everything blurs as we're evaluated and loaded into an ambulance, and the next thing I know, we're speeding toward the Fillmore Hospital.

I have an urge to tell the paramedic that the driver might want to slow down. The roads are really wet.

Often we think of a book as a movie that runs through our minds, but it is more effective to think of a novel as a stage production. We, the authors, are the producers and must provide the proper lighting, music, and sets to support the plot and create a perfect scene. Every element of description should be active in conveying the mood and essential framework of your plot.

We can create a multi-dimensional experience for our readers by weaving careful, intentional description in our work.

Stop and Smell the Roses: Sensory Writing

This may come as something of a surprise to you, but unless you're writing about an alien species with limited sensory receptors, your characters have bodies.

Shocking, I know.

They are not just a set of eyes floating around within the walls of your written pages. To better simulate real life, writers must use that nose, that mouth, those hands and feet to help characters—and vicariously readers—experience the world around them.

Good description opens a door for readers to cross the boundary from observer to participant. It grants them access to not only "see the movie" but to feel the brush of the wind on their cheeks, to imagine the numbing sensation of walking barefoot in a mountain stream, and to experience the tender nuances of a first kiss.

Description is what makes books so much better than movies. Because not only are we seeing, touching, tasting, and hearing the world through the main character's eyes, we also get to understand, on an intimate level, what those sensations inspire in the character emotionally.

Smells especially have the ability to transport a character to a memory that provides a key window into their past. A character might smell a pair of old boots and crinkle his nose while thinking of a beloved father who passed only last year. Nostalgia can be a powerful writing tool!

How often do you walk into the forest without running your hands along the pine needles of a tree and smelling the lemongrass growing wild in the underbrush? When was the last time you went to a beach without walking barefoot in the sand or tasting the salt of the ocean while playing in the surf? And yet so often we limit our readers' experiences to only what our characters can see.

These moments are missed opportunities.

I often encourage young writers to examine a chapter of their book and highlight the different uses of the senses in their writing, with the exception of sight.

You might find that it's a rather surprising experiment.

Great story crafters are not necessarily master poets. It may take some practice for you to get in the habit of writing using all of the senses. I highly recommend sensory writing prompts for this reason.

Try writing a list of all of the scene locations featured in your story. If you write contemporary fiction, your list may look something like this:

- Bedroom
- City Library
- Train Station
- Christmas tree lot
- Coffee shop
- Jail

I like to write these locations on strips of paper, fold them, and place them in a bowl on my writing desk. Every time I sit down to write, I'll draw a slip and imagine the following:

"If my character were blindfolded going into this scene, what senses would they have to rely upon? Knowing what I do about their past, how would the character describe this setting?"

I then do a free write for five minutes. The time goes by fast and I'm always surprised by the awesome descriptions lurking in the cobwebs of my mind.

There is a false belief that good writers are just gifted individuals who see the world in unique ways. I disagree. Though we may have varying aptitudes when it comes to creativity, I sincerely believe that artists and creators grow into talented professionals in two different ways:

1. They give their minds permission to ponder and wonder.
2. They practice.

Writing with the senses may at first be a challenge, but with patience and *practice* you will find that the descriptions will come a little easier every time. Your mind will transport you to the awesome place where your muse connects with the tips of your fingers (if you're typing) and the words just seem to flow.

> **Travel Log Note**: In Greek mythology, a muse is one of the nine women responsible for creating the arts. In today's culture, it is a term for anything that provides inspiration. It's also a '90s British rock band that put out several good songs. "Uprising" is probably my favorite, if you want to check them out.

British rock band Muse

Creating a Mood

As I mentioned at the beginning of this chapter, carefully crafted description can help transport your reader into the story. It can also strongly hint at the emotion and mood of a scene.

Too often writers take a wrong turn when they attempt to describe feelings and emotion. They use *telling* words such as "feel" and "was" and tack on a weak *telling* adjective like scared, happy, curious, angry, etc.

Describe a forest

Anytime a writer tells the reader how a character is feeling, we have a missed opportunity to bring the reader into the story. Writers should strive to *show* feelings through action and description. We'll discuss editing for these missed opportunities more in the next chapter. For now, let's practice bringing emotion into description so that messy habit of *telling* can be avoided.

Imagine the protagonist of your story walking down this path in the woods. I'm sure you could come up with a hundred different descriptive ways to paint the scene for your reader. Here's the question: Would the descriptions change depending on the mood you're hoping to set?

Answer: IT TOTALLY SHOULD!

If you are describing the setting depicted in this picture during a lover's walk, you might point out the warmth of the sun as it filters through the trees, the smell of the loam soil after a light rain, a breeze causing the leaves to tremble in anticipation… You get the idea.

Let's use that same picture and pretend our character has just escaped the clutches of a sinister villain and is racing down this wooded trail to safety. What would the character notice in that scene? Without saying "he was terrified," how could we convey the fear of the moment?

I would focus more on the dead leaves crunching beneath his feet, the gnarled branches reaching out to slow his escape. I'd have my character noticing more of the shadows of the forest instead of the light.

The same picture, but two different moods generated with careful description. We never have to come out and say "she was happy" or "he was scared" because our characters are going to notice the items around them that reflect their mood and then communicate that mood to the reader through their actions and dialogue.

By setting the mood, the reader has the opportunity to draw their own conclusions. We're building tension by letting them predict the outcome of a scene based on the description offered. It is a subtle practice that provides a masterful touch to storytelling and truly sets the amateur and professional apart.

Similes and Metaphors

I love writing similes and metaphors because they have the ability to convey a lot with very few words. Just as a review:

A *simile* is a comparison using the words "like" or "as."
> Example 1: The lion was as tame as a kitten.
> Example 2: Life is like a box of chocolates.

> **Travel Log Note**: This second example is a quote from one of the greatest movies of all time! *Forrest Gump* came out in 1994 and was one of the most heavily quoted and viewed movies of the decade. If I had a nickel for every time someone said, "Jenny, why won't you marry me…?" (That will make sense if you take my advice and watch the movie.)

A *metaphor* is a straight comparison between two things.
> Example 1: Life is a highway.
> Example 2: Love is a battlefield.

There really is nothing like a powerful simile or metaphor, but they come with a few potholes if you aren't careful. Here are my top three points of advice when dealing with similes and metaphors:

1.   Beware the over-use of similes and metaphors. They will start to lose their power if your manuscript is saturated with them. Take this passage, for instance:

> *He was a fox in a hen house, and she needed to get away before he could hurt her again. You can't love a dragon, no matter how much you try.*

Here the subject of the passage is referred to as both a fox and a dragon. When very different comparisons are made back-to-back, it's called a *mixed metaphor*. It is far better to use one simile or metaphor at a time, and then elaborate and strengthen the description surrounding it rather than to dilute the metaphor with a second comparison that has no relation to the first.

2.   Avoid cliché comparisons. Think of a cliché as a common saying that you might hear/read all the time, such as:

- par for the course
- avoid him like the plague
- angry as a bear
- right as rain
- strong as an ox
- light as a feather
- black as night

When describing a character's emotions or situation, cliché comparisons are unimaginative and tend to become a little obnoxious to the reader. Another problem with clichés is they are so common, they don't inspire thought or feeling in the reader. Descriptions should always max out the emotion of the scene, and clichés are just fluff. Remember, metaphors/similes provide an opportunity to be creative.

3.   Liken the metaphor/simile to the narrator.

In the movie *Shrek*, Shrek opens up to Donkey, explaining that he's more than just a mean, green villain. He uses the simile, "Ogres are like onions" to explain that there are layers to his character. Donkey doesn't like the comparison and wants him to say instead that he is like a parfait because "everyone likes a good parfait."

Writers must beware turning into the Donkey of this situation. When selecting a metaphor or simile, we must keep in mind the speaker or narrator whose perspective you're writing from.

In one of my books I have a character who works as a blacksmith. When he speaks, I want his dialogue to reflect the influences of his life. His tone is rough. He often uses analogies about iron ore, hammers, and fire. A seamstress, on the other hand, would likely see the world through the lens of her experience with thread, patterns, and needles.

Consider your characters as you craft your description. They will help you avoid common cliché comparisons and give you the creative boost you need.

Physical Description: Do's and Don'ts

Providing physical description for your characters should be a strategic decision for an author. First, you must decide exactly how much detail you want to provide to your readers and how much of the physical makeup of the character you want to leave in the care of your readers' imagination. Second, you'll have to decide how the reader learns these details. This can be especially tricky if you're writing a book in first person POV.

> **Travel Log Note**: I review first person POV in detail in Chapter 1.

Remember, the key is to be creative. Please, please don't begin a character description by only focusing on hair and eye color. How many times have you read about a touch of gold rimming blue or green or brown eyes or hair cascading around a woman's shoulders? Instead of focusing on the obvious, why not select a more creative physical feature—something that creates a window into the character's personality?

Hands tell a lot about a person. Consider the graceful curve of a pianist's fingers, or the ever-present paint on the back of an artist's hand, the calluses of the rock climber, and the steady hands of a surgeon.

Posture conveys a great deal about a character's mood, education, and profession. Lips can be full and pouting or thin and shapeless. Shoulders can be boney or broad. Long torsos, short legs, small noses, high foreheads, heart-shaped faces. Do you see how many ways there are to describe a character without being cliché and only providing information on eyes and hair?

I travel a lot, and one of my favorite pastimes is people-watching. I'll sit in an airport and study a person, trying to dissect the perfect and most unique way to describe them. It's a lot of fun… until you get caught staring. Then it can be a little awkward. ☺

Hit the Road: Description Writing Prompt

Part One: List the different scene locations found in your book and write the following:
1. How can you describe the scene using senses beyond just sight?
2. What details would your character notice that reflect his/her mood?

Part Two: Go to a public place such as a park, library, or grocery store and list descriptions you might use to capture a person's physical appearance without mentioning hair or eye color.

8

Construction Zone: Editing in Progress

The fly taunts my kid sister, Haley, like a big brother with ADHD. She swats and whines and rolls down the window in our parents' SUV to coax it out, but with no success.

It's a nice day in June. The weather is warm and pleasant as I test my newly acquired driving skills on the Alpine Highway. The freedom of transportation sparks a distinct feeling of adulthood and I want to share this new independence with my younger sisters by treating them to a movie.

"I can't get it out!" Haley cries.

I am the big sister. I am a driver now. I can handle a pesky fly.

The Suburban is big, so I have to lean over quite a bit to assist with the shooing of the fly. I look up just in time to see the mail car parked on the side of the road. I tug on the steering wheel, but it's too late. Metal screeches against metal and all the Eldredge girls scream as we sideswipe the postal truck.

I right the SUV and we don't stop. It takes me at least two football fields to realize that I should pull over. I'm too afraid to make a U-turn, so with shaking hands I park and step out of the car onto my jelly legs. My walk back to the crash site turns into a full-out sprint as I consider the fact that I may have actually hurt someone. I'm a terrible person.

The cherries and blueberries of the cop car are flashing when I finally get to the sad-looking postal truck. A worker in USPS blues is cupping the back of her neck and a police officer reports a hit-and-run into his radio.

"I'm here!" I half pant, half shout. My hands rest on my knees as I catch my breath. "This is all my fault."

Well, *I think to myself.* Mine and the fly's.

Fines Double for Speeding

Like any teenager, I couldn't wait for the day to get my license. I woke up on my sixteenth birthday and arrived at the DMV five minutes before they opened. Even when I had my license, I enthusiastically drove wherever I went, resulting in two speeding tickets and the lovely accident with the fly.

Often writers approach their manuscripts with the same gusto. They toil and sweat over the first draft of a story only to speed through a quick round of edits and revision.

Every author has their own process for taking an idea and transforming it into a book polished enough to enter the publishing market. Some people plot, some write by the seat of their pants; some can get a first draft out in a matter of weeks, and others take five years. No matter the type of writer, one step that every author absolutely can't bypass is editing.

Even the most inspired books written by the most experienced authors benefit from polishing. So how does one take a first draft and transform it into a shining, professional masterpiece?

I like to take the following steps:

Step One: The chapter-by-chapter content analysis

In this step, I read each chapter of the book searching for ways to improve some of the "big picture" aspects of the story. I read to improve characterization by seeking opportunities to plant questions and pique curiosity in my readers. I challenge the characters' physical descriptions to ensure I'm showing my readers a unique, strategic window into their true selves.

I'll also use this read to determine the strength of my setting. Every writer is different. While I do a decent job providing the framework of my setting in the first draft, it is during the chapter-by-chapter analysis that I add little details that make the story transform from an idea to a complete "breathing" scene for my characters to move within.

The content analysis is a great time to do the *tension testing* discussed in Chapter 5 of this book.

This step is also a great time to make big changes to the plot, discard full scenes, and write new ones. If you approach this phase of editing as though every word in the book is expendable, you open yourself up to some amazing story ideas you may have not considered before. The moment you're afraid to sacrifice a line, paragraph, or even a full chapter is the moment your story stops growing and evolving into something better.

In his fantastic book *On Writing,* Stephen King refers to willingness to eliminate characters, scenes, etc., as "killing your darlings." Sometimes we become attached to a beautifully written passage that doesn't fit perfectly into the puzzle of the plot. Professional writers have to axe great words all the time. It's part of the job. I sometimes create a "cut file" to store all of my "darlings" just in case I find a place to use them somewhere else in the story. It rarely happens, but it makes it easier to cut passages I love when I know they exist somewhere.

Travel Log Note: Leave it to a horror writer like Stephen King to paint a mental picture of murdering pages. The creative author in me can't get that image of someone driving a knife through a book out of my head whenever I hear this expression.

Step Two: Enlist beta readers

Once I feel pretty confident about the content of a book, I'll take the sometimes-scary step of giving it over to people I can trust to give me honest feedback. In other words, I avoid giving it to family or friends who will say everything that I write is packed with glitter and roses. As nice as it is to hear positive feedback, a shower of praise will not improve my manuscript.

Because finding people to read your work can be tricky, I highly recommend finding a writers group of about three to six writers to swap manuscripts. I go in depth about writers groups in the next chapter.

Before I hand my manuscript over to a beta reader, I construct a list of questions and concerns about the story. I try not to allow my questions to influence the reading, so I sometimes add questions at the end of certain chapters, or even the end of the book.

I make it very clear to my beta readers about the type of critique I'm hoping for. I ask them not to worry about grammatical errors because I will catch those in later rounds of edits. With my beta readers, I'm only concerned about the core facets of the story: plot, character, setting, tension, etc.

Examples of questions I might ask my beta reader include:

1. What are your impressions of the main character? What do you like? Dislike?
2. Do you have any predictions about the villain or main conflict of the story at this point?
3. How could I make this a more satisfying resolution?

Whether you're using a word processor or an online file, ask the reader to add comments in the file, offering impressions and reactions. It helps me to know if they think something is gross or funny, or if they dislike a character or description. I always ask my readers to highlight sentences that made them stop and re-read. This quick action on their part will help speed along my next round of edits.

It is important that you have at least two or three people read the book before you move on from this phase in the editing process. You may find that what bothers one person is another person's favorite aspect of the book. Everyone is different, and you don't have to agree with everyone's opinion. Keep in mind that if you notice something is bothering more than one reader, it is definitely something you should consider revising.

Travel Log Note: Actions speak louder than words. I can always tell if a trusted beta reader likes my book by the amount of time they take to read it. If they turn it around quickly, that tells me the tension and pacing of the story is good. If they take longer than usual, then I can assume there are a few slow areas in the book, and I'll be sure to ask the reader to point them out to me.

Step Three: Review feedback and revise

Once you receive feedback from your beta readers, first look for any large plot issues mentioned in your critique. I recommend working on those issues first because there is no sense in editing chapters if you plan to cut or add large chunks of words later.

A word of caution: You will likely feel tempted to settle with the book as it is. Often the idea of making big changes can be daunting. Biting the bullet and making those changes is something that separates great authors from amateurs. Persevere!

Once I've addressed the big picture edits, then I go from chapter to chapter incorporating the minor edits and suggestions from my beta readers.

For example, if I have three beta readers for a project, I'll pull up the file from each reader and minimize them on my desktop. I'll scan through the first reader's comments for chapter one, then go back to my master copy and make the appropriate changes. If I'm uncertain about an editorial suggestion, I'll flag it in my master file. I'll then move on to comments from my second reader for chapter one and repeat the process.

I will not move on to the next chapter in a book until I've addressed all of the feedback received in the first chapter.

Step Four: The Line Edit

What's a line edit? Just as the name implies, it involves a taking a close look at every sentence of the novel, editing for grammar, word choice, and sentence structure.

Before I jump in to this step, I've found that it's helpful to take a little break from the manuscript. Read a book. Write something totally different for a week or two. Basically, step away long enough to refresh your "editing eyes." You know the book so well, you can read it with your eyes closed. This makes it difficult to catch errors before your brain autocorrects them.

Once you've taken some time off and you're ready to dig in to the nitty-gritty edits of the book, you'll want to check for the following:

Edit for Passive Voice & Inactive Writing

What is passive voice? Good question. Passive voice refers to the word choice an author uses in both dialogue and narration. When we speak or write passively, we tend to add words that slow down or muddy the reading experience. I remember learning in school that if you can insert the phrase "by zombies" after a phrase, it's likely passive.

Example:

English is being studied ~~by Ali.~~ by zombies!

The word "being" is also a good sign that this sentence is passive. Here is a more active way to say the same thing:

English is studied by Ali.

Better, right? But it's not quite there. Active voice (vs. passive voice) uses the fewest words possible to pack the biggest punch. The previous sentence is five words long. We can tighten it even more by simply stating:

Ali studies English.

Here are some real-life edits from one of my own manuscripts:

The gaps in the shutters allowed light to filter into the room.

This isn't a terrible sentence, but we can make it more active by cutting words and starting with the subject.

Light filtered through the gaps in the shutters.

We just cut four words and the narration flows much smoother, the message more direct and clear.

> **Travel Log Note**: "If I had more time, I'd write you a shorter letter." This is a common quote used by authors and no one can agree on its origins. Some think it was first written by the famous philosopher John Locke; others give credit to Benjamin Franklin. Winston Churchill has been quoted for similar statements as well—my favorite (and likely the most inappropriate) being, "We will do our best and try to make this column like a woman's skirt: short enough to be attractive, but long enough to cover the subject."

Another way to spot inactive writing is to look for areas in your writing that "tell" the reader what is happening and how the characters respond instead of "showing" them the action through active narration. This is also discussed with relation to writing description in Chapter 7.

Here's another real-life edit from one of my own manuscripts:

Captain Jobrad was furious when he saw the chest of money was stolen.

You can usually recognize *telling* when you see any of these words in a sentence followed by emotion:
- Felt
- Was
- Were

I call these "missed opportunity words" because they lead to weak writing. Remember, I want to *show* my readers that Jobrad was furious. Let's make that sentence more active:

When Jobrad discovered the money missing, he slit a deckhand's throat.

Not only do we get to experience Jobrad's anger in this sentence, we learn what the man is capable of doing to his own men. Characterization! This is the power of active voice and showing vs. telling.

Edit for Redundancies

It takes much longer to write a chapter than it does to read it. Because of this, authors tend not to notice repeating words and phrases that disrupt the reading experience. Anything that pulls the reader out of the story is a big problem and repeated words and phrases tend to make the reader pause and think, *They just said that.*

If you're writing a scene that takes place in a mountain stream, you may accidently use the word "water" three times in a paragraph without even noticing it. You may have a go-to phrase you weren't even aware of that pops up a few times throughout a chapter. Or you may forget the way you described someone's expression at the beginning of the book and give that exact same description later on. Repeating the same metaphor is a redundancy that also pulls a reader out of a story.

Editing for redundancies can be difficult because the author's word choices within a single sentence may be perfectly fine. The problem only exists when those words and sentences string together in a paragraph, chapter, and full book.

The best way to catch these errors is to read your manuscript aloud or to use a program that will read text back to you. The voice may be robotic, but that is generally how I catch sneaky repeats in my writing.

Edit for POV Changes and Tense Changes

Staying consistent with point of view and tense is, without question, the biggest struggle young authors make. Many are avid readers. They jump from book to book reading narration in past and present tense, first and third person POV, and find themselves mimicking the writing style of the latest book they just read. During your line editing phase, take extra care to stay consistent with both POV and tense. This will help your reader avoid confusion and sink into the story.

> **Travel Log Note**: See Chapter 1 for a review on Tense and POV.

Edit for Cliché Phrases

Have you ever heard any of these phrases?

- Actions speak louder than words.
- The grass is always greener on the other side.
- The apple doesn't fall far from the tree.
- You can't judge a book by its cover.
- You can't please everyone.
- What doesn't kill you makes you stronger.
- Love is blind.
- Ignorance is bliss.

Though these familiar sayings might be used in common speech, it's important to avoid them in writing. You want your work to sound fresh and original, and using cliché phrases and descriptions tends to cheapen the writing, giving the impression the writer was too lazy to be creative. If you happen to find a cliché phrase while editing, turn on that creative brain of yours and think up your own description—something that fits the context of the scene/character.

Edit for Sentence Variation

Pay attention to the length and structure of your sentences. Beautifully written prose use varying sentence lengths and types to entice the reader, speed up or slow down a moment, and add a lyrical cadence to the writing. Shorter sentences tend to reduce complexity and clarify meaning while longer sentences can add emphasis to a thought or description.

Gary Provost is famous for writing this example of the importance of sentence variation:

"This sentence has five words. Here are five more words. Five-word sentences are fine. But several together become monotonous. Listen to

what is happening. The writing is getting boring. The sound of it drones. It's like a stuck record. The ear demands some variety.

Now listen. I vary the sentence length, and I create music. Music. The writing sings. It has a pleasant rhythm, a lilt, a harmony. I use short sentences. And I use sentences of medium length. And sometimes, when I am certain the reader is rested, I will engage him with a sentence of considerable length, a sentence that burns with energy and builds with all the impetus of a crescendo, the roll of the drums, the crash of the cymbals— sounds that say listen to this, it is important."

Compare the repetition of the five-word sentences of the first paragraph to the variety provided by the second paragraph. Which writing style do you prefer?

Obviously, the latter.

Length is not the only factor to consider. There are three very common sentence patterns from which you might choose.

> **Travel Log Note**: Don't panic with you see some of these grammatical terms! I remember my mind switching off in school whenever I heard big words like coordinating conjunction, insubordinate clause, etc. The "wah wah wah" of the teacher in Charlie Brown replaced all logical words in my fuzzy brain. For the sake of your writing, don't give up on me!

1. The Simple Sentence

This sentence contains one independent clause (a phrase that has a subject and verb) or a subject and predicate (action) that can stand on its own.

Examples:
- *I tried to shoo a fly from my car.*
- *Crash!*
- *My car struck the side of the mail truck with shocking force.*
- *It took a long time for my brain to process what had just happened.*
- *I cried.*

- *The police gave me a ticket for speeding.*

Notice how the length of a simple sentence can vary? It can even be just one word so long as both the subject (noun) and the action (verb) of the sentence are implied.

2. The Compound Sentence

Compound sentences are formed by linking two independent clauses with a conjunction (for, and, nor, but, or, yet, so).

Examples:

- *I ran back to the scene of the crash, and I told the policewoman a fly was to blame.*
- *She gave me a ticket for speeding, but I was too grateful no one was hurt to care.*
- *I'd only had my license for two weeks, so I doubted my parents would ever trust me again with the family car.*

3. The Complex Sentence

Complex sentences contain an independent clause and a dependent clause that cannot stand on its own. You'll often find the words "because" or "while" connecting the two clauses.

Examples:

- *Because of my accident, I learned that flies are dumb.*
- *They should be exterminated from the face of the planet, while I sit back and gloat over their gruesome deaths.*
- *Though I may never drive again, I can rest easier knowing the population of this destructive insect will suffer!*

One last trick to help vary your sentences is to simply change the sentence beginning. If all of your sentences begin with the words I, the, it, or this, then they will bore your reader to tears. Mix it up! Consider occasionally beginning your sentences with adverbs or actions.

Hit the Road: Test Your Inner Editor
Writing Prompt

Part One: Read the passage below and edit it for
1. Passive voice and inactive writing
2. Point of view switches
3. Changes in tense
4. Word and phrase redundancies
5. Cliché phrases

(Hint: There is at least one error from each of the categories listed above.)

The Suburban is big, so I have to lean over quite a bit to assist with the shooing of the fly. I looked up just in time to see the mail car parked on the side of the road. My heart stops. I tug on the steering wheel, but it's too late. Metal is screeching against metal and all the Eldredge girls screech as we sideswipe the postal truck.

She decides to right the SUV and they don't stop. It takes me at least two football fields to realize that I should pull over. I'm too afraid to make a U-turn, so with shaking hands I parked and step out of the car onto my shaking legs. My walk back to the crash site turned into a full-out sprint as I considered the fact that I may have actually hurt someone. I'm a terrible person.

Part Two: Take the first chapter of your book and conduct a line edit for the following:
1. Passive voice
2. Point of view switches
3. Changes in tense
4. Word and phrase redundancies
5. Cliché phrases
6. Sentence Variation

9

Navigating Detours and Going the Distance

This was all my fault. I knew when we agreed to drive with Beau that there was a good chance we'd run in to something like this. This wasn't the first time we had to get creative to start Beau's car—no connecting jumper cables or changing the oil for this fix.

"I can't help you tonight, dude." I point to my 99-cent flip-flops. They're about as durable as crepe paper and they've already broken once tonight.

"Just take 'em off."

I narrow my eyes. This is an old neighborhood with rough roads in need of resurfacing. I have tough feet, but even my calluses can't save me from the damage this road will inflict.

Complaining is fruitless. Beau is my ride home. No one has a cell phone and we definitely don't have money.

"Let's just get this over with." I sigh, throwing my ratty shoes into the front passenger seat of the car.

Beau climbs into the driver's seat and puts the car in neutral while two of my friends and I push his rolling hunk of metal out into the road. I'm grateful that it's late and no cars are in sight. Small mercies.

Once the car is positioned on its "run way," we take a moment to catch our breath.

Beau is a good guy, and it was nice of him to drive, especially since I was completely out of gas and funds. Next time, I just need to remember to wear the proper footwear.

Reaching over, Beau rolls down the passenger-side window so I have a better grip for pushing. Our friend Brett positions himself at the back since he's the real muscle of this operation. It's the trickiest position because it requires the most running after *the car starts.*

"Have I mentioned that I like you?" asks Beau.

I roll my eyes. He always gets sentimental when his car makes him rely on the charity of others. "Let's just get this thing started."

Brett provides the countdown, as if we're a bobsled team preparing for push-off. "Three, two, one!"

We dig in, pushing the little car with all we have. Once we get the metal monster rolling, it's easier to build up speed. My feet burn beneath me as we run.

"Pop the clutch!" Brett calls.

Beau obeys and the car sputters and shakes before the soft purr of the engine gives us the cue to jump in. Running alongside the car, I grab the latch and pull the passenger door open. Pain knifes through the pad of my foot just as I launch myself into the car feet first and slam the door behind me. The two rear doors shut and we're off.

Beau's car rattles as he shifts into a higher gear. He grins, as though proud of himself even though we did the hard work.

I lift up my foot, propping it on my opposite knee to investigate the damage.

A piece of glass the size of a quarter dangles from my flesh. Blood drips onto the seat of the car and I cringe. "Got any napkins?"

"Are you bleeding on my car?" Beau asks.

I glare at him in response and he throws his hands up in a surrendered apology.

The cut is deep and I know it needs cleaning.

We roll to a stop at a red light. Beau throws the car into neutral and revs the gas. "Glove box."

I find the napkins and even an old band-aid. Judging by the yellowed wrapper, I'm guessing it belonged to the original car owner (circa 1979).

Good enough for me.

The light turns green and right when Beau puts the car into gear, the engine sputters and dies.

"You're killing me!" I growl.

The rear doors open as my friends get out to help. For a second, I consider sitting this one out, but I know how hard it is to get this hunk of metal moving with just one person sitting in the car.

"Have I ever told you how much I like you?" Beau asks again.

This earns another eye roll from me. "Let's just do this."

I will never forget the most important, meaningful day of my writing career. I remember hitting the return key on my computer keyboard and staring at the blinking cursor. The words I'd been striving to write ever since typing the first page of my very first novel vibrated on the tips of my fingers. I drew them out, hitting each key with finality and conviction. An entire year's worth of work had brought me to that moment, and I wanted every letter to count.

T-H-E... E-N-D

I remember clicking the Save button, closing my laptop, and squealing. Snatching up my one-year-old, I ran through the entire main floor of the house shouting, "YESSSSSSS!" My toddler ran after me, laughing at the game I'd invented. The baby started to cry and I suddenly realized there were tears in my eyes, too. Not the "my mom is losing her mind" tears, but tears of relief and joy. I had set a hard goal for myself—one I almost abandoned on more than one occasion—and I had just slayed the dragon.

Victory was mine.

I was an official author.

I remembering thinking that fame and fortune would soon follow. All that remained was to quickly snatch up a killer literary agent and to master my signature for the millions of copies I'd be signing that time next year.

To this day, my first novel is probably the most personal, important book I've ever written. It represented the first of many "word marathons" I would run over the course of my publishing career. The story was original, creative, and packed with loveable characters who deserved a chance to live through the pages on my manuscript.

So, what happened next?

How did my publishing story play out?

Like so many characters in books, I had to endure my fair share of conflict and rejection before anyone in the publishing industry started saying yes to my work. At every proverbial stoplight, it felt like I was running on glass with no clear victory in sight.

Throughout this chapter I'll paint you a detailed picture of the steps to become a traditionally published author and provide some commentary about my experience with each step along the way.

Before we jump into that process, I think it's important to drive home one underlying requirement for all authors with publishing aspirations.

Writing is something the author can control. We control when we sit down to our computer, what goes into the story, who we show the manuscript to once we've finished that first draft, etc.

In publishing, the author hands over a great deal of control to someone else. As much as we all wish it were possible, the author cannot determine who will love their work, where or if it will be published, how many people will read it, how readers will react to the story, etc. Authors also have very little say in design decisions regarding cover and layout, when the book will publish, how a publisher markets the book, etc.

It is so important that you, as a writer, set goals for yourself, but the goal should never involve things outside your own control.

When I first started writing at age twenty-five, I set a goal that I wanted to be published by the time I was thirty. It was a lovely idea, but every time I received another rejection, every year my birthday came without a book deal, I sank deeper and deeper into misery. I was so hard on myself, feeling as though I was a worthless hack that would never amount to anything.

What I failed to realize is that the writing itself was all that mattered.

I didn't sell that first book. I didn't even come close to getting a literary agent with that book.

Thankfully, I kept writing. I finished a second novel and submitted at least forty query letters to different agents around the publishing industry trying to get someone to look at my work. I remember feeling so small, like I was an ant screaming at the world, "Give me a chance!" No one could hear me.

I'd once heard that it takes writing a thousand bad pages before one can start writing good pages. I had more stories to tell, and despite my pitiful responses and countless rewrites, I knew I couldn't give up on my dream of becoming a professional writer. It wasn't until I'd started writing my third book that an agent contacted me asking to represent my second novel.

To say I was thrilled was a gross understatement.

I'd arrived! I was validated! This whole writing thing was a good idea after all! I could do this!

But no one told me that having an agent wouldn't guarantee a book deal. I knew it might take time, but surly great things were in my future.

A year passed and the book never sold. My agent sent me emails from bigtime editors saying how much they loved the voice of my characters. However, the book was too whimsical to fit in the edgy young adult market and too mature for the middle grade genre.

I was crushed. How cruel of the publishing gods to taunt me with the hope of success, to bring me right to the waters of awesomeness and not let me drink from the pool. Cruel.

My agent asked if I had anything else she might shop. I'd been working on my third book, but it was different from anything else my agent had submitted to editors previously. I didn't know if I could handle much more rejection.

My agent loved the book and after a few months of edits and submissions, it found a home with my very first publishing house.

I was thirty-one years old when my third book, *Nameless*, sold.

I tell you my story because I firmly believe writers should have reasonable expectations when approaching this career path. Publishing trends come and go. Great books don't always sell. Brilliant authors don't always publish. If you learn anything from this book, please let it be this:

THE MERIT OF A WRITER IS NOT MEASURED BY A PUBLISHING DEAL.

A writer's value is measured by their commitment to developing the writing craft and the bravery and beauty of daring to create.

Now that I have that off my chest, let's talk traditional publishing…

The Road to Traditional Publishing

By way of introduction, you should know that large publishers almost never accept submissions directly from authors. Authors must first obtain a literary agent who has developed relationships with publishers.

What does a literary agent do?

They act as the gateway between the author and the publisher. They negotiate contracts, pitch books, and look out for the rights of their clients (the authors). Agents often have specific genres they prefer to work with and develop relationships with editors at various publishing houses who acquire, or buy the rights to, books in their genre.

What is an editor?

Editors work for publishing houses. They are the big dogs you need to impress if you want to get a book deal. If they like your book, they'll often take it back to a committee and convince the publisher your project is right for the publishing house.

It sounds like a lot of hoops to jump through… mostly because it is.

Before you can even think about getting that big publishing contract, you first must go through these five steps.

Step One: Write an Amazing Book

Publishers are looking for something they can sell. They want something that is original that will stand out on a bookshelf, a concept no one has done before.

In Mark Twain's autobiography he wrote, "There is no such thing as a new idea. It is impossible. We simply take a lot of old ideas and put them into a sort of mental kaleidoscope. We give them a turn and they make new and curious combinations. We keep on turning and making new combinations indefinitely, but they are the same old pieces of colored glass that have been in use through all the ages."

Revenge, love, betrayal, fear, honor—all are old concepts reproduced and recycled countless times. But your "combination of colors" should provide a new way of experiencing those classic themes.

Once you've finished writing the book, have sent it to beta readers, completed several rounds of revisions, and feel the book is as clean as you can possibly make it, then it's time to move on to step two.

Step Two: Creating the Pitch Package

I know so many authors who excel at writing but struggle when it comes to preparing materials to help them pitch their book. For many writers, they are so emotionally attached to the project that fear of putting their "baby" out into the world to face critics and rejection is simply too much for them. They freeze in the face of rejection and forget that pitching a book to industry professionals is all about expressing that initial passion for the story that they felt in the early stages of writing the book.

Authors should ask themselves the question, "What excites me about this book?" Your answer is very likely the element of intrigue that will hook a potential agent/editor.

What is a pitch package? It's basically the submission materials a literary agent requests from authors who want to be represented by their agency. Submission requirements vary from agent to agent and editor to editor, but one thing every agent and editor will require is a query letter.

I think of a query letter as an audition of sorts designed to ignite interest in both a story and its author. Agents and editors have a pile of submissions on their plate, and they want to know right away if the book is in their preferred genre with around the right wordcount before they want to move on to the rest of the pitch. Therefore, state the total word count and genre in the introduction of the query letter.

Dear [Agent's Name],

TAKE A CHANCE ON ME is a young adult contemporary novel complete at 80,000 words.

Notice I mentioned that the book is complete. Agents and editors have absolutely no interest in taking on a work of fiction if it is not complete.

Next, I recommend including a one-to-three paragraph pitch of the book. The art of writing a pitch can be very tricky. Not only do you want them to fall in love with your story, you are essentially showing the agent/editor that you are a wordsmith by the way you condense the book into a tight ball.

The query pitch must accomplish the following:

1. Introduce the protagonist and antagonist of the story by showing us what they want (motivation again!) and why.
2. Hint at the action. If the protagonist is crossing the Rocky Mountains to escape a zombie army, then mention rock climbing, cliffs, and wild animals. If there is a love interest, definitely sell that to the agent/editor. Consider your book as a movie trailer. What details would a producer show to "sell" the movie to potential audiences? If there is humor, action, and epic love in the plot, you can bet we'll see a glimpse of that action in the trailer. The same should be true for the book pitch.
3. Explain what will happen if the characters fail. What is at stake?

Here is a pitch I recently wrote for my latest project:

Would you touch the one you loved, even if it might kill them?

Fina Perona is cursed; terrible things happen to anyone who touches her skin. Overcome with guilt when Fina's curse kills her most beloved brother, she flees her family's vineyard and takes to the seas only to be caught in a terrible storm. Her boat capsizes and Antonio, a young merchant sailor, saves her from drowning, inadvertently linking their fates.

Fina learns Antonio's ship is en route back to the home she just aban-doned, carrying desperately needed payment for her father's prized wine stores. Pirates attack, and as Antonio and Fina escape the clutches of slavery, she steals back her family's small fortune from the captain's quar-ters. Fina doesn't need Antonio's protection—she's more dangerous than he could ever be—but she needs his experience as a navigator and agrees to accept his help in exchange for a cut. Returning the money is the only way she knows how to atone for her brother's death, but what she doesn't realize is, before Antonio was a sailor, he was a thief.

While the threats of curses, witches, bandits, pirates, and traitors are all very real, Fina and Antonio are the most dangerous players in this game. Will they become each other's demise or salvation as they set out to find redemption and to kill a curse?

Notice that I didn't give away the ending? In a query, that is com-pletely acceptable and often the common practice.

The final element of the query is nearly as important as the pitch. This paragraph introduces the author (that's you) and convinces the agent/editor that you are the right person to write this particular book. This section can be extremely intimidating for many writers without publishing credentials, but get creative. If the hero of the story is a blacksmith, ex-plain the research that has gone into learning the craft.

For the story I pitched above, I interviewed seasoned sailors and went out onto the high seas myself to crew a small sailing vessel to get an idea of how to write that lifestyle and describe the inspiration for writing the story. These are great details to include in this paragraph. Obviously, if you have any college degrees or writing awards or accolades, this would be a great time to mention them.

Travel Log Note: "Write what you know" is a common saying in the publishing world. I don't necessarily agree with this adage, but I do agree that writers have a responsibility to do their research. I can't tell you how many documentaries I've watched to understand cultures, weaponry, crafts, etc., so that I can accurately portray characters and cultures in my writing. It's fun to learn new things!

Step Three: Researching Agents and Editors

Anyone can type "How do I find a literary agent?" into a search engine and come up with some respectable sources for agent hunting. The most common resources I recommend are Writers Marketplace (which requires a paid subscription) and QueryTracker.com (free). Both databases are popular with agents and have search filters that help you connect with agents interested in exactly what you write. There are definitely other resources out there, but it's important to remember that not every agent is going to be the right fit for you and your work. Remember how the first thing an agent wants to know is your genre? If you submit a query for your romance novel to an agent who specializes in Sci-Fi, you won't be successful. Do your research. Know your genre and search for agents who are seeking exactly what you write.

Another way to find an agent is to find a recently published book similar in genre and audience to your own. Take a moment to turn to the Acknowledgements located at the back or front of the book. Agents are almost always mentioned.

Once you compile a good list of agents who have recently sold books in your genre, take the time to visit each of their websites. They will usually post if they are accepting "unsolicited submissions." This means they will take a look at your stuff even if you have not been personally invited to send something to them.

Take notes on each agent's submission guidelines. They all might want something different. For example, one agent might ask you to send a one-page synopsis. Another might just require a query and the first chapter. It is important to send an agent only what they ask for—nothing more, nothing less. Double-check the spelling of their name. You don't want to kill an opportunity because you get sloppy at the finish line. I also recommend writing a list of the books they've sold over the past five years. If they haven't found much recent success, this should be a warning sign that perhaps they aren't in a position to sell your book to a publisher.

Be warned: You should never, ever pay money for a literary agent. They receive payment when they sell your book. The standard rate for an agent is 15% on domestic sales (United States) and 20% on foreign sales. If you notice an agent asking for money upfront, you should run in the other direction. They're likely scamming you.

As I mentioned before, the only time you will ever contact a publishing house directly is if they are a smaller publisher and if you have a vast knowledge of publishing contacts. There are a number of indie publishers that accept unsolicited submissions. If you do decide to submit directly to a publisher, I recommend following the same steps that you would with an agent. First, research the publisher and their submission guidelines, then follow their guidelines to the letter.

Step Four: Forming a Submission Plan

Once I've done all of my research and have created a strong list of literary agents, I like to arrange them in order from least to greatest based on my desire to work with them. I determine this by the amount of success they are having, the books they've represented, and how well my manuscript matches their interests.

I work through my list from bottom to top, starting with the least and moving to that dream agent. I prepare a submission for five to ten agents at a time and send them my "baby." Then I wait about a month for a response before submitting to the next agents on my list.

You can learn a lot about your query, synopsis, and first few chapters by what happens (or doesn't happen) next.

1. No response can mean
   a. They aren't looking for what I sent them
   b. My query didn't grab them.
   c. They simply haven't had a chance to read it yet.

Agent and publisher websites will usually say how long authors can expect to wait before they receive a response. Once that time has passed, wait one more week and then send a follow-up email asking if they've had a chance to review your query. Be sure to include the date of your original submission so they know you aren't just nagging them.

2. I loved it but…
   a. Whatever comes after that "but" is golden! It may be a clue to help you tighten your submission package or story. Just remember, it is one person's opinion.
   b. You might find that they "loved it, but already have something similar they are trying to shop." Any rejection is tough, but this is more of a "it's not you, it's me" rejection.

3. Generic rejection letter or "form rejection"
   a. These are the rejections that bother me the most because it's impossible to know if the rejection comes because the agent/editor is simply not inspired by the writing, they aren't seeking projects in your genre, or they simply are just too busy to take on more clients. You'll never know.

Travel Log Note: The worst rejection I ever received came from an agent who told me that "perhaps writing is just not for you." I remember shaking my fist at the sky and pounding out 2,000 words that day just to prove that he was wrong. Rejection is hard, but it can also be quite motivating.

Step Five: Hurry Up and Wait

Once your submissions are out, the healthiest thing you can do is immediately start writing a new project. If a writer's greatest desire is to be published and the book they're trying to sell is the first of a series, I strongly recommend taking a break from writing in that world. It may take years to publish your first book, and if you're like most authors, your first book may never sell. Your creative brain has had to walk through the dreary mires of publishing a novel—a very left-brained process that few authors enjoy. Reward your efforts with a fresh new world, characters, and ideas. This a great way to keep you in "writing shape" and fuel the passion of storytelling.

The most important goal a writer can have is to improve their craft. It's something that is not dependent on the whims of the publishing industry and can be obtained by hard work from the author. If you are fortunate enough to sell a book in your lifetime, fantastic! But making publishing the goal will likely prove discouraging. Creative writing is a form of art. The artist paints for commission, but they first paint for the challenge and satisfaction of producing something beautiful. Of expressing one's self.

Publishing is a byproduct, not the ultimate goal.

The Self-Publishing Pros and Cons

As a traditionally published author, I do not consider myself an expert on the intricacies of self-publishing. However, I can help you understand the motivations behind those that prefer this option and help you decide if it is right for you.

Self-publishing is a great option for authors who don't want to wait for the slow publishing industry to get their book out into the world. These authors are usually not afraid of learning new things and have a good mind for business and marketing. Because a publisher's primary job is to market and help produce a professional literary product, the self-publisher must wear the hat of author, editor, designer, marketer, and accountant.

It's difficult to stand out in this very competitive industry, so if that is your goal, plan on doing your research and devoting a great deal of time (and resources) to marketing. Often authors will hire others to produce a cover and edit the book. If an author devotes enough energy into this effort, they can find success, but it does usually take multiple books published and a little bit of luck to start making money.

One of the greatest appeals to self-publishing is creative control. In traditional publishing the author has very little say in the cover design and often is asked to make changes in the book with which they don't fully agree. In self-publishing, the author calls all the shots.

Hit the Road: Goals beyond Publishing
Writing Prompt

Part One: Analyze your writing goals. Write at least three obtainable goals for your writing that can be measured and achieved without the validation or acceptance of others. For example, publishing should not be the goal because it relies on someone else's acceptance.

Part Two: Write a query letter for your own manuscript *or* for a book you love.

A Note to Teachers

Huzzah! I love English/creative writing teachers and what they represent in education. Many of the students that walk through the doors of your classrooms have always associated writing with a grade. They've been trained from a young age to produce the right words following the proper format.

It is my hope that this book inspires your students to color outside the lines, challenge basic ideas, and discover a deeper level of creativity of which they never knew they were capable. Sadly, public education requires benchmarks, grades, and standardization that tend to narrow the creative arts.

I've included the chart below to help English teachers "justify" the time they spend encouraging their student to push creative boundaries. The Hit the Road exercises found at the end of each chapter are designed to fulfill national Common Core standards in grades 6 through 12. These writing activities are a great way to measure effort and motivate your students while fostering the creativity that will follow them out of your classroom and into boardrooms, engineering firms, operating rooms, etc.

I firmly believe that *all* success is rooted in creativity of some form.

Thank you for giving these teens permission to create and the tools of self-expression that will have a lasting impact on their lives.

Common Core Writing Standards for 6th -12th Grade in correlation with Teen Writer's Guide:

Grade	Ch.1	Ch. 2	Ch. 3	Ch. 4	Ch. 5	Ch.6	Ch. 7	Ch. 8
6th-8th	3.a, 3.b	3.a, 3.b	3.a, 3.c	3.a, 3.b	3.b	3.b	3.b, 3.d	3.c
9th-10th	3.a	3.a, 3.b	3.a	3.a, 3.b, 3.c	3.b	3.b	3.b, 3.d	3.d, 5
11th-12th	3.a	3.a, 3.b	3.a	3.a, 3.b, 3.c	3.b, 3.c	3.b	3.b, 3.d	3.d, 5

About the Author

With her degree in history and secondary education, Jennifer Jenkins had every intention of teaching teens to love George Washington, the Napoleonic Wars, and ancient Sparta… until the writing began. She is the author of the Nameless trilogy (YA fantasy) and the Lingering Sea Trilogy (adult fantasy). She is also a co-founder of Teen Author Boot Camp, a 501c3 non-profit organization dedicated to promoting teen literacy and authorship.

She divides her free time between reading, writing music for piano and guitar, taking spontaneous trips, researching random events from the past, and fostering her adrenaline junkie addictions (mountain biking, trail running, competitive backyard soccer ☺, hockey, snow and water skiing, hiking, kayaking, horseback riding, (and really anything else that helps her forget she turned thirty-something this year.) She is the mother of three awesome kids and is married to the most supportive man on the planet.

Notable items yet to be checked off her bucket list are 1) being called "lass" in an Irish pub, 2) dancing with a man in breeches, and 3) watching an episode of Seinfeld without cracking up.

Find Jennifer online at
www.authorjenniferjenkins.com

Acknowledgements

In the aftermath of World War II, Welsh poet, Dylan Thomas, wrote a poem that would forever solidify his career as a poet and writer. The poem *Do not go gentle into that great light* was more than just a message to Dylan's dying father; it was a plea to fight against good things that fade and die.

As both a teacher and lover of the written word, it has been my mission, long before my first novel ever sold, to preserve the teaching of creative writing in public schools. With the introduction of the national common core and major cuts in the arts, creative writing is just one of the outlets often sacrificed on the altars of "new education" in public schools today. With the help of some extremely talented, motivated friends, we formed a 501c3 nonprofit to foster creative writing and teen authorship in our local community, state, and nation. Teen Author Boot Camp is the flagship of that endeavor, and I have to acknowledge Margie Jordan, Tahsha Wilson, Jo Schaffer-Layton, and Lois D. Brown for all of their help in providing literally thousands of teens the chance to develop powerful skills of self-expression. This effort, more than any other, has been the highlight of my career, and the motivation behind the book you now hold in your hands. With these women, we've fought to "Rage, rage against the dying light."

It has bonded us in ways nothing else could. I love you. It has been an honor.

I have to acknowledge Amy Jameson for encouraging me to write this book and Olivia Swenson for her editing prowess. Special thanks to the Owl Hollow Press team and my "renaissance woman" publisher, Emma Nelson, for believing in the project and developing such a gorgeous cover. The book is lovely and you are lovely. I also need to thank the following beta readers: Amy Beatty, Nichole Van, Lois D. Brown, Dr. Rosalyn Eves, Kathryn Purdie, and Jessica Day George. Your insights have been priceless.

I'm so grateful to my loving parents who not only supplied writing fodder for this book, but also encouraged and praised my writing as a teen. I firmly believe I never would have fallen in love with story and the written word without your influence and cheerleading. My siblings, also, make a few appearances in this work. They are foundational in my life. Thanks to Josh, Whitney, Haley, Joseph, and Savannah. It's been one heck of a ride. Glad to have shared many memorable journeys with you.

I am forever grateful to my little family. Casey, Lib, and Boss, you are the engine behind everything I do. Clint, you are the fuel that keeps me rolling. I love you all.

To the teens I've had the good fortune of teaching and mentoring over the years: I am both amazed and inspired by you. "*Do not go gentle into that great light.*"

Photo Credits

Page	Description	Source
8	Manarola, Italy	Jennifer Jenkins, 2013.
27	Beeper/Pager	"29 Images That Perfectly Explain What The '90s Were Like" https://www.buzzfeed.com/juliegerstein/29-images-that-anyone-who-was-a-teen-in-the-90s-will-recognize
28	Willie Nelson	"Willie Nelson's Outlaw Music Festival" https://consequenceofsound.net/2019/03/willie-nelson-outlaw-festival-lineup/
29	Jennifer Jenkins' father	BYU Athletic Department, 1982.
45	Hurricane view	NASA Worldview. Public Domain, 1992.
46	Aftermath, Hurricane Andrew	Mark Foley, Associated Press. http://today.com/story/news/2017/08/24/hurricane-andrew-haunts-florida-25-years-later/577624001, 1992.
64	Road Closed Sign	Jennifer Jenkins, 2017.

64	Movie Set Saloon	Taken for Jennifer Jenkins by unknown individual, 2017.
116	Muse	IMDB, https://www.imdb.com/name/nm0615614/
117	Forest of trees	Pixabay, Royalty Free image, https://cdn.pixabay.com/photo/2016/09/01/21/43/forest-1637686_960_720.jpg
127	Book stabbed with knife	Trent Johnson. On Tap Magazine. http://ontaponline.com/event/murder-mansion-dessert-theater/book-stabbed-with-knife, 2017.
157	Author headshot	NicholeV Photography

Hey, teen writer!
Want to become a published author?

Every year Owl Hollow Press and Teen Author Boot Camp team up for a teen-only anthology. Follow us on social media to be in the loop when we announce the next deadline and theme.

Until then, check out our past anthologies by teen writers, just like you!

Band of Misfits: Adventure on the High Seas
    foreword by NYT bestselling author Kiersten White
Join our Clan
    foreword by NYT bestselling author Jennifer A. Nielsen
Choose Your Own Adventure
    foreword by Colorado Book Award winning author Darby Karchut

Website: owlhollowpress.com
Twitter: @owlhollowpress
Facebook: Owl Hollow Press
Instagram: owlhollowpress

OWL HOLLOW PRESS
WORLD-ALTERING STORIES, REAL AND IMAGINED

CPSIA information can be obtained
at www.ICGtesting.com
Printed in the USA
LVHW100856180920
666362LV00007B/389